FIRESIDE CHATS

FIRESIDE CHATS
A TREASURY OF INSPIRATION

DAN HARLESS

BAKER BOOK HOUSE, Grand Rapids, Michigan

for
Lady Claire

Copyright 1974 by
Baker Book House Company
ISBN: 0-8010-4103-1
Library of Congress
Catalog Card Number: 74-20201
Printed in the United States of America

Foreword

As I read the manuscript of *Fireside Chats, A Treasury of Inspiration*, I enjoyed many a laugh, and occasionally I felt a tear. These fireside chats are intimate little essays which have something in common with *Aesop's Fables* and the old *McGuffey Readers* in their beneficial effects.

The ultimate message of the book is preeminently Christian, with illustrations and quotations from the Bible serving as a foundation for everything else. The book is unusually thought-provoking. The author is one of the most widely-read men that I have known, and he punctuates his sketches with apt quotations and illustrations from history, the arts, literature, science, and current affairs. In this day when so many of us are so rushed that we have little time to read, except in a surface way, it is deeply rewarding to be able to enjoy the fruits of another's wide reading. Personal observations and experiences give a rich dimension to the sketches.

All of this would be relatively tasteless if the book were put together in a dull, methodical, ordinary way—which definitely is not the case with this book. The style — imaginative, vivid, witty, and even brilliant — makes the sketches enjoyable reading. There is a scholarliness about them, but also simplicity and freshness. The author is preeminently a writer, one with a rare gift for using words skilfully and effectively.

Dan Harless is a man of wide experience. He is a Christian gentleman and is married to a lovely Christian lady — literally — Lady Claire. They have five children, a daughter and four sons, the youngest being twins. Together they constitute a warm, loving, wonderful family.

Life has not always been easy for Dan Harless. While there have been mountain peaks, there have also been valleys, and some of these have been quite deep. Some people would have been overwhelmed, but not this man. He has demonstrated inner spiritual strength, maturity, and courage. He is a man of wisdom, sympathy, and understanding. With it all there is a perpetual cheerfulness. Everyone who knows him likes him, especially those who know him best.

I predict that, as you read these fireside chats, there will be enjoyment, the stirring of the emotions, stimulation to a better way of life, and new insights concerning some of the problems that face us personally and nationally. There is also likely to be a deep self-examination, which is all too rare in this hurried age. Most important of all, as the Biblical themes appear throughout, the reader will be drawn closer to his Lord.

— Batsell Barrett Baxter

Contents

Courage

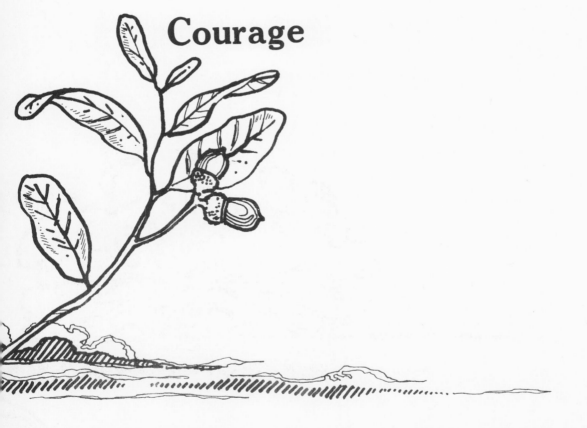

Just Like a Man

Most of us, at one time or another, feel quite sure we have all the answers (provided, of course, that we are not on the receiving end of the questions. It's an entirely different matter when we find ourselves pinned down. Answers are hard to come by at such times). This presumption is a common failing, one that has been going on for a long, long time. For example, in the Book of Job, thought by some scholars to be the oldest book in the Bible, we find that even Job stumbled over that false assumption. In his presumptuousness he was positive that he knew all the answers. "Oh, that I knew where I might find him," he said, "I would set my cause in order before him, and fill my mouth with arguments. I would know the words which he would answer me, and understand what he would say unto me."

That was pretty strong language. Some time later the Lord answered Job, instructing him to "gird up now thy loins like a man." I suppose in modern speech the Lord's charge would read, "Stand up on your feet like a man." That, of course, is what the Lord has required in every age, men who are willing to stand up on their own two feet. Then the Lord asked Job some forty questions. Job, who thought he knew all the answers, couldn't answer even one question.

These days attention is often directed to the foibles of the male of the species by the question, "Isn't that just like a man?" So what's wrong with acting like a man?

Johnny Cardwell was the hard luck champion of his school . . . broke his leg in football practice . . . disqualified after winning the mile run because he stepped out of his lane before the first turn . . . dropped the baton in the relay. Johnny continued his hard luck routine after he finished school. You name it, Johnny had first hand information about it . . . pneumonia one year, a slipped disc the next . . . a break-in at his store one week and a fire a few days later. And so it went.

One day his friend Pete, who was visiting Johnny in the hospital, brought up the subject. "Look here, Johnny," he said, "you're a magnet for trouble. How do you keep from letting all these things get you down?" Johnny grinned and said something about all the little things that had happened to him just might make him strong enough to withstand real trouble if it ever came his way. "But, Johnny," Pete protested, "don't you think you've had real trouble? What about the time. . . ."

Johnny cut him off with a wave of his hand. "Pete, I thought one time I was in serious trouble. I didn't know which way to turn. That's when I happened to read where the Lord told Job to stand up on his feet and be a man. Well, I guess that's what I've been trying to do ever since."

Johnny's outlook on life calls to mind another Bible statement. It's found in Paul's first letter to the Corinthians: "Watch ye, stand fast in the faith, ACT LIKE MEN, be strong." That's great advice for men (and women) in these disturbing times.

CJ

Carrie Jo was born and reared in a southern college town. Her parents were wealthy and they saw nothing wrong in indulging their only daughter. In spite of their lack of prudence, CJ, as she was known affectionately by her friends, was unaffected by their adoring solicitude.

CJ was quite an athlete. She captured the girls' tennis singles title during her junior and senior years in high school. By the time she entered her junior year in college she was being touted for the national championship.

If CJ had an enemy, she wasn't aware of it. Her sunny disposition caused her to be voted "most popular girl" in her senior year. She planned to devote one year to serious tennis competition and after that — well, a certain young intern would be putting up his shingle and she had promised she would be his "till death do us part."

But it was not to be. CJ came home from a tournament feeling, as she said, "perfectly awful." The doctor gave her something to ease the pain and suggested she go to the hospital for a day or so in order that he might run some tests. That was the beginning of the end. Beautiful, vivacious CJ was hardly recognizable when she was released from the hospital about a month later. The doctors diagnosed her case as one of those unpronounceable, very rare, and always fatal diseases.

CJ's friends suffered agonies when they saw her weaving awkwardly down the street, stumbling, and sometimes falling. She had always looked as though she had just finished dressing for a beauty contest. Now her dress was baggy and often twisted, her shoes were scuffed, and her once shining hair hung limp and lusterless. But some things about CJ remained exactly the same. Her smile, her spirit, and her magnificent courage: in these there was no change.

One day, toward the end when CJ was back in the hospital, the preacher spoke to her feelingly about her amazing fortitude. CJ's reply was somewhat enigmatic. She said, "It's just that I know about the swelling of Jordan now." When he looked puzzled she said softly, "You know . . . Jeremiah the twelfth chapter . . ." Her voice faded away.

About that passage in Jeremiah: It reads, "If thou hast run with the footmen, and they have wearied thee, then how canst thou contend with horses? And if in the land of peace, wherein thou trustedst, they wearied thee, then how wilt thou do in the swelling of Jordan?" A good question. CJ found the answer. How about you?

Growing Old

Old Dr. Dean was a powerhouse in his day. As a matter of fact, he is still doing pretty well for a man his age. But everyone, everyone but Dr. Dean, knew he is going downhill. Last week, Dr. Dean admitted this fact of nature himself.

Doc stopped in to see Jim Fletcher one morning. Jim had a virus infection and Doc told him to stay in bed, to take his medicine, and he then would be all right in a few days. He quoted that old saw about obeying doctor's orders so that he would be well in seven days — otherwise it would take a week.

Sally Fletcher insisted that Doc stay for breakfast. "If you don't, you'll eat some of that horrible stuff they serve down at the Greasy Spoon," Sally said. Doc's wife had been gone now for more than a year.

Doc grumbled and snorted but he sat down and stowed away some sizable portions of pancakes and sausage. As he was having his second cup of coffee, Doc started talking about how soft folks are nowadays. "They get old before their time," he insisted. "Now take me, I'm not going to get old."

Jim, Jr., aged ten, looked up at Doc's wrinkled face and observed innocently, "But you did."

Sally became flustered and began hustling Jim off to school. Old Doc's face turned beet red.

When Sally came back into the room, nervous and apologetic, Doc said, "Look here, Sally, there's no need for you to fret about Jimmy when he tells the truth. I've been trying to kid myself for years that the old clock won't ever run down. But like Jimmy says, I've grown old. Yep, I've grown old in spite of everything."

Dr. Dean isn't the only one who has had to face up to advancing age. That's something we all have to do. And chances are, for a lot of us, it's later than we think.

It's hard to grow old gracefully and bravely. There's more to it than merely coping with increasing aches and pains. There is the matter of acquiring a spiritual outlook. This is an absolute necessity if we would avoid "having eyes that seeth not."

We read of David that he "died in a good old age, full of days and honor." But length isn't all there is to life. There is breadth, depth, and height, as well as length. When a man has all four, he has everything he needs.

When Moses was a hundred and twenty years old he delivered this charge to Israel: "Be strong and of good courage . . . the Lord your God . . . goes with you, he will not fail you or forsake you; do not fear or be dismayed" (Deut. 31:6, 8). That's a mighty fine passage to think about when, like Doc Dean, we must face up to the fact that old age has caught up with us.

Blind Eddie

Eddie lost his sight during his junior year in high school. Eddie was one of the most promising track stars in the entire history of Central High. And now Eddie couldn't even watch the sport he loved with a passion.

But that didn't stop Eddie. He prevailed on Coach Jimmy Brown to let him run the 440, on the outside lane, making use of a specially constructed guide wire.

Eddie didn't do very well at first. Having to put out his hand to touch the wire every few steps upset his rhythm and his arm movements were no longer free and flowing. But Eddie kept at it. He came in third in one meet and second in another. The doctor said it wouldn't hurt him physically and it would do a great deal for him mentally.

The coach didn't look for Eddie in his senior year. It took a lot of hard study, with Eddie's mother and sister reading to him, to get by. But Eddie came out. This time he was much more confident. As for training, he practically wore out that wire. He regained his rhythm and his stride was something beautiful to see.

Because he needed to use the guide wire, Eddie competed only in the meets held at Central. And he burned up the track in every meet. But it was the state meet, held at Central that year, that was unforgettable. In the finals Eddie was running against top competitors from all over the state. When the starter's gun cracked, Eddie shot out in front. He ran like a frightened deer. The crowd broke loose and pressed along the finish line. Everybody wanted to see the finish line. And that's where it happened — at the finish line. The crowd kept building up until those in front were pushed against Eddie's guide wire. The wire came down and Eddie tripped over it, right at the tape.

You can imagine what a tumble he took. But he also took first place. The spectators were contrite and solicitous now. They backed off to give Coach Brown room as he rushed over to help Eddie to his feet. But Eddie didn't need any help. He jumped up, blood streaming from cuts and cinders clinging to his face and hands and knees. "I can see," he shouted, "I can see!" The crowd was silent for a moment and then a deafening roar went up.

A long time ago in Palestine another man who had been blind shouted, "Now I can see!" The Great Physician later commented to His disciples: "Blessed are your eyes for they see." But He wasn't talking about physical eyes. How about you, do you have 20/20 spiritual vision?

Thorns

Sam was the world's leading hard luck man — to hear Sam tell it. Sam could and did ask all and sundry why things had to happen to him as they did, why he came down with a cold on the night his singing group was scheduled to give a program, why he had to lose a tooth on the night of the company banquet, why? *why?* WHY!

There never were any really big things, no hardships beyond the normal disappointments common to everybody, but Sam really moaned and groaned about everything.

And then one day Sam was driving home from the office, thinking about a fishing trip. He and Bill planned to leave at four the next morning. Sam never saw or heard the car that hit him. When he regained consciousness hours later, he was so swathed in bandages that he was unable to move.

Well, there was no fishing trip that week, or the next, or the next. For all Sam knew, there never would be again. With his wife Lucy sitting by the bed, Sam asked the doctor to let him have it straight. How bad off was he? The doctor told him. Sam might not walk again.

Sam closed his eyes. Thoughts raced through his head. What about his job? his family? his new home? new car? investments that needed watching? Yes, and what about his life? Sam was in real trouble. For the first time in his life he had something to moan about.

A week or so later Sam was sitting up in bed reading. Someone had left a basket of fruit and neatly tucked away in the basket was a New Testament. The night before, Sam had been reading the twelfth chapter of II Corinthians. He was puzzled over Paul's reference to his thorn in the flesh. Sam read the passage again: "By reason of the exceeding greatness of the revelations, that I should not be exalted overmuch, there was given to me a thorn in the flesh, a messenger of Satan to buffet me, that I should not be exalted overmuch. Concerning this thing I besought the Lord thrice, that it might depart from me. And he hath said unto me, My grace is sufficient for thee: for my power is made perfect in weaknesses, that the power of Christ may rest upon me. Wherefore I take pleasure in weaknesses, in injuries, in necessities, in persecutions, in distresses, for Christ's sake for when I am weak, then am I strong."

Sam slowly read the words again, "a thorn in the flesh . . . I besought the Lord . . . My grace is sufficient for thee . . . my power is made perfect in weakness. . . ." He closed the book. There was a look of resolution on his face. Sam muttered, "His grace is sufficient for me, too."

When the doctor and Lucy came by a moment later Sam appeared to be asleep, but he heard these reassuring words:

"I talked with the specialist this morning," the doctor said to Lucy. "Sam's going to be all right. What he needs most of all is to relax, to get plenty of sleep, and let nature do her work. He'll walk. It will take time and determination, but he's going to walk. He'll make it just fine."

If a Man Die

Yesterday I stopped by the hospital to see Tom Carver.
Tom won't be with us long and he knows it. After the usual
small talk, Tom said, "I have just read a question in the
Bible. It's in the fourteenth chapter of Job." He hesitated
a moment and then he said, with a note of pleading in his
voice, "I wonder if you can give me an answer?"

Tom handed me his Bible. It was open and the place was
marked: "If a man die, shall he live again?" At that point
I breathed a silent prayer of thanks for having studied
this absorbing question and for having memorized the
Scripture verses where the answers to Job's question are found.

I began with Paul's words in I Corinthians 15:50-57
about the inability of flesh and blood to inherit the kingdom
of heaven and Christ's victory over death. Then there are
other answers to that perplexing problem: "I know that
my redeemer liveth, and that he shall stand at the latter
day upon the earth" (Job 19:25, *KJV*). "I know whom I have
believed, and am persuaded that he is able to keep
that which I have committed unto him against that day"
(II Tim. 1:12, *KJV*). "To him that overcometh will I grant to sit
with me in my throne" (Rev. 3:21, *KJV*). "I am the resurrection,
and the life: he that believeth in me, though he were dead,
yet shall he live: and whosover liveth and believeth in
me shall never die" (John 11:25, 26, *KJV*).

I know these readings helped Tom. I know they helped me
because "I *know* that my Redeemer liveth." I *know* he
is the "true resurrection and the life."

Aunt Jeannie

"How could God do this to me?" That's what pretty Linda Smith asked everybody who visited her in the hospital after the auto wreck. Linda wasn't pretty any more. Her face was a horrible caricature of a once-lovely, beautifully complexioned girl. Her attitude wasn't pretty either; it was in keeping with her poor, battered features. She was fast becoming a miserable shrew.

Old Mrs. Hagood, Aunt Jeannie, as she was affectionately known by everybody in town, dropped by to see Linda. And that marked the beginning of Linda's first faltering steps on the long come-back trail.

"Hello, child," Aunt Jeannie greeted Linda in her bluff, hearty way. And then she came out with a barrage of questions: "How long have you been crying? Do you think you've got it out of your system? Do you want to hear some good news? Are you going to be a real woman, or are you planning to bemoan your fate for the rest of your days?"

Molly Jordan, who was fussing and fixing around Linda's bed and clicking her tongue sympathetically every time Linda moaned, looked now as if she might have a stroke.

But Linda opened her eyes and said, "Aunt Jeannie, what do you have to tell me?"

Aunt Jeannie sat down, opened her ample purse, and took out a worn, dog-eared Bible. Adjusting her glasses, she turned and read these words: "Grace is deceitful, and beauty is vain; but a woman that feareth Jehovah, she shall be praised."

"Did you know these words were written about three thousand years ago by the wisest man who ever lived?" she asked. "And now," she said, fixing Linda in her gaze, "I want you to listen carefully."

Linda listened. And Aunt Jeannie talked, for a long time. She talked about Linda's facial scars and she talked about even worse scars, the kind that disfigure the mind and spirit. She insisted that Linda's life was not over; it was just beginning, and only Linda could make it burdensome or beautiful. Then Aunt Jeannie wound up by quoting the words of David: "Let the beauty of the Lord our God be upon us."

This all happened a long time ago. Linda's blithe spirit has brought joy to others as it brought to Linda herself an inner radiance. Aunt Jeannie is gone but her brave words and influence linger on.

A Tip for the Waiter

Eddie and Jean came from a small town and both were working in the big city. The going had been rough but things had taken a sudden upward turn. Eddie was called to the office. The boss complimented Eddie and broke the news of his promotion and the whopping increase in salary that went with it.

This called for a celebration, with Jean of course. Eddie knew the very place, a beautiful restaurant that served marvelous food at unbelievably high prices. But this, Eddie reasoned, was special.

As Eddie and Jean savored the beautiful decor, snowy cloth, exquisite tableware, as well as the gourmet food, they found themselves in a blissful state of love's young dream. Jean had never been more beautiful. Eddie had never appeared more dashing and handsome. Eddie's hand closed over Jean's as he said, "Why can't we be married right away?" Jean's adorable smile lighted up her face as she said, "No reason at all, except one little thing."

"What do you mean? What little thing?"

"Well," Jean said mischievously, "you haven't asked me yet."

At that moment the waiter walked up. He looked down on the youngsters with a blasé, world-weary air, made an inquiry as to whether they had enjoyed their dinner, and then launched into a story which, he said, another customer had just told him. The story was off-color. It brought Eddie and Jean back to earth with a thump. Jean was embarrassed and Eddie was boiling. He would have reprimanded the waiter sharply but he didn't want to make matters worse for Jean.

Thoughtfully, Eddie counted out the exact amount of the tab. Then he took out his pen and wrote on the back of a card, "Tip for the waiter: The words of the apostle Paul to all men everywhere, including waiters, 'Let no corrupt speech proceed out of your mouth, but such as is good for edifying as the need may be, that it may give grace to them that hear.'" Then he underscored *Ephesians 4:20*.

The Whistler

I was soaked to the skin the other night but I hardly noticed it until my wife smilingly remarked that she had heard of people who didn't know enough to come in out of the rain.

It was about 8:30 and I was hurrying to get home before the storm broke. It reminded me of the weather in England when I was stationed there during the war. Just as I was passing the little cottage where old Mr. Archer lives, I heard his stereo going full blast. He was a concert violinist before he injured his hands. The music was the familiar second movement of Tchaikovsky's Fifth Symphony. The music carried me back over the years; I did not notice when the rain started.

It was on a dark, stormy night in London during the blitz. I was young and scared and lost — couldn't see my hand in front of my face and I was late for an important meeting. That was when I heard the whistler. I never did learn his name. He was whistling that same tune from the second movement from Tchaikovsky's Fifth. Strange thing — he was walking at a brisk pace. Just as he was about to brush by I asked if he could direct me to a famous Downing Street address.

"Quite. Come along," he said in his precise, clipped accent, "it's nearby."

I had difficulty keeping up because I still could not see. Finally I blurted, "Say, I can't see; you'll have to slow down."

"Just take my arm, old chap," he said.

I took his arm. In two or three minutes he said, "Here you are. See you again."

He started to move off but I held his arm. "Tell me," I asked, "do you have some kind of second sight? How can you see in the dark?"

"Ah, yes," he said, "that does make a difference doesn't it? That is to you, but not to me. You see, old chap, I'm blind. Well, good luck." And with that he was off, whistling. I stood there until I could no longer hear him, then I turned and went into headquarters.

So the other evening I just stood in front of the Archer place listening. Later, as we were having family devotions, our Jimmy read from the thirteenth chapter of Matthew: "This people's heart is waxed gross, and their ears are dull of hearing, and their eyes they have closed; lest haply they should perceive with their eyes, and hear with their ears, and understand with their heart, and should turn again, and I should heal them. But blessed are your eyes, for they see."

Lynn

It's hard to believe that we'll never hear Lynn Larimore's low chuckle any more. Lynn died last week. What a loss. Not for Lynn. She was ready to go; but, oh, what a loss for everybody who knew her.

A group of us got together for coffee after the funeral. In spite of the sadness of the occasion we couldn't help laughing every now and then when someone would say, "And do you remember the time Lynn. . . ." And then some lively, heartwarming story would recapture for a moment Lynn's gaiety and sparkle.

Someone asked, "Just what was it that Lynn had that made her so happy?"

A good question. Just what did she have? Well, she had a chronic heart condition for one thing. And she was burdened financially trying to put her young brother through college. Then there was the matter of a terrific car wreck. After months in the hospital and several operations she was able to get around but she was in constant pain. "Most anybody else in her condition," Doc Hanson said, "would have wound up on drugs." But if Doc hadn't mentioned it, nobody would have learned from Lynn that she was having any difficulty.

It's pretty obvious that Lynn had some inner power that kept her spirits high. While we were talking, young Eddie, Lynn's brother, came in. He saw us and came to our table. His smile was just like Lynn's. We exchanged a few words and then Joe Benson told Eddie we had been talking about Lynn's marvelous disposition and about how much we had admired her.

Eddie took a card from his billfold. "In case you're wondering how it was my sister never let things get her down, I have the answer on this card. She sent it to me during my first year at the university and insisted that I carry it with me at all times. She carried one just like it in her purse."

Eddie handed the card to Joe. Joe read it aloud: "I can do all things through Christ who strengtheneth me."

The Lynn Larimores of this world serve to remind us of one of the most important teachings of our Lord: "My strength is made perfect in weakness."

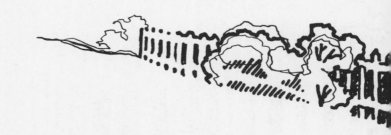

People

Down in the Back

Pat Jenkins played eighteen holes of golf one day last month. This was unusual. Ordinarily when Pat plays he doesn't stop short of twenty-seven. However, on that day last month he said he was "down in the back." Pat hasn't played since. Nor will he ever play again.

Pat and his friends were on the fourteenth tee when he felt a twinge in his back. He parred the hole and in spite of increasing pain he continued through the eighteenth.

The next day he had considerable difficulty getting out of bed. At the office he limped around and parried the good natured thrusts of his fellow workers. "Yeah," Pat replied in answer to Jack Fowler's gibes, "I guess I wrenched my back when I picked up a marshmallow."

Two days later Pat decided to see a doctor. It was no longer a joking matter. The pain was far worse. Waves of excruciating pain engulfed him at times. The doctor put him through a series of X-rays. Pat nearly fainted getting on and off the table.

The following day more X-rays were taken. Pat surmised that there was something seriously wrong. But Pat's diagnosis was a little short. It was not merely serious; it was critical.

What had been merely an ugly word to Pat was now a dreadful reality. Cancer! Pat sensed how difficult it was for Doc Thompson to admit it was inoperable. Doc's face was as tired and drawn as if he were the patient himself. The verdict was extremely painful to Doc and absolutely shattering to Pat.

There are many Pat Jenkins in this world and there must of necessity be Doc Thompsons on hand to break the distressing news.

When I heard about Pat, my heart went out to him, to his lovely wife, and to his children. Also, I found it difficult to put away the thought that the cancer of sin continues to creep into the lives of millions.

One of these days medical science may triumph over cancer. As for sin, there is healing only in the treatment prescribed by God's Son, the Great Physician.

Euphemism

A euphemism, according to Webster, is "the substitution of a mild or indirect word or expression for one unpleasant or offensive, though more accurate."

"Though more accurate." That portion of the definition came back to me the other day when I was visiting in the lovely country home of a friend.

Picture if you will a cold rainy day. Flames are dancing and crackling on the hearth. Guests are sitting and walking about engaged in pleasant conversation as they enjoy the warmth of the fire and each other's company.

Pal, the big, long-haired, slew-footed family pet slips in as the door is left unguarded. Pal has been chasing rabbits. He has swum in the creek. He has been in the barn with the cattle. He has had an unfortunate encounter with a skunk. Pal's fragrance is something less desirable than Chanel #5.

One lady comments on Pal's noble bearing. A gentleman remarks on the dog's past exploits. But a little boy gets a whiff of Pal and says, "Pal, get out of this house; you stink!" The boy has grasped the situation at a glance, at a whiff that is, and his reaction is spontaneous, logical, and to the point. He doesn't know anything about the polite world of euphemisms. Nor does he say, "Pal, dear canis familiaris, your odoriferousness in such close contiguity to my olfactory organs is somewhat unpleasant." Instead, with admirable directness, he says simply, "Pal, you stink!"

Genuine Christians have a similar childlike quality. They refuse to go along with labeling fornication as an affair, or calling prostitutes party girls, or drunkenness a facet of generous living, or lying a form of diplomacy, or stealing a demonstration of ingenuity. Nor did Jesus mince words. He said, "He that believeth not shall be condemned." And, on another occasion, "Except you repent, you shall perish." Nothing euphemistic there!

Standard of Measurement

Frank Fisher is an electrical engineer. He is proud of his profession and he is proud of having graduated from M.I.T.

Fisher is an intense, hard-driving man. He is somewhat of a mathematical wizard. The new systems, about which there has been so much publicity, are quite simple and logical to Frank Fisher. It isn't unusual for him to whip out his slide rule or pocket computer and solve a knotty problem while others are still wondering how to start. Problems just don't get too big for Fisher — except one.

The new preacher came by to pay his respects one evening. Fisher's wife served coffee and then sat in fear of some horrendous argument her husband might drag out to engulf and confuse the poor parson.

Before the preacher could invite Fisher to church the engineer said something like this: "Now I want you to know, preacher, that I've never studied the Bible but I think whatever a man believes is all right and it makes no difference if he accepts or rejects the Bible or if he makes up a set of rules for himself. Religion, as I see it, is a matter of following anything that appeals to the individual and gives him a sense of well-being."

The preacher looked over his glasses and said mildly, "I'm sure your outlook covers every phase of your life."

"Certainly," Fisher snapped, "It's the only way a man can meet the complexities of our age."

"I see," the preacher said musingly, "you feel, then, that no standard of measurement is needed for religion. Right?"

"Right," Fisher said emphatically.

"May I see that slide rule sticking out of your pocket?" the preacher asked.

"You know anything about a slide rule?" asked Fisher, patronizingly.

"Oh, yes, everything."

"No kidding! everything?"

"Of course," the preacher said, "I've never studied one. In fact, this is the first time I've ever had one in my hand. But every man's entitled to his belief. I think we should have all kinds of rules in order to fit our personal preferences in mathematics. Now this business of having twelve inches to a foot — I think it would be much better to have eleven or thirteen or however many one might choose. Mr. Fisher, don't you think we should follow the rule, or as in this case the slide-rule, of our choice?"

Fisher didn't reply for some time as the seconds ticked away. Finally he grinned and said, "Touché preacher: I'm coming down Sunday and hear you preach."

It was the apostle Paul who said, "Let us walk by the same rule, let us mind the same thing" (Phil. 3:16).

Timid Terry

During his school days Terry was a first string fullback. Somebody said "When Terry hits, they stay hit and when Terry tackles, they stay tackled." He was also on the track team. He broke the school shot put record by a full twelve inches his first time out. Terry was quite a man, but he was so shy that even ordinary conversations were painful ordeals for him.

There was the time, following an undefeated season, when Terry was called on to make a speech. He managed to raise his ponderous bulk away from the table, but he was unable to utter a word. After a long, agonized silence, he waved feebly and sat down.

The other day I sat listening to a handsome, articulate lawyer speaking in behalf of a measure designed to improve city government. The speaker was none other than Terrence Worthington, alias Timid Terry.

Later, while we were having lunch, I asked Terry how he had managed to overcome his shyness and develop into such an accomplished speaker. Without a trace of embarrassment Terry fished into his attache case and pulled out a well-worn Bible.

"I'm sure you remember that time at the school banquet when I couldn't say a word," Terry said. "Well, I decided that night that something had to be done. The first thing I did was to pray. And then I began to read this book. There were so many things that seemed to point to me and to my problem, especially in the Book of Proverbs. But this is what did the trick. Let me read it to you."

"The fear of man bringeth a snare: but whoso putteth his trust in the Lord shall be safe" (Prov. 29:25, *KJV*).

The Square

"The integrity of the upright shall guide them; but the perverseness of the treacherous shall destroy them." These words were written by Solomon nearly three thousand years ago. I saw the quotation recently. It was on the inside cover of a chemistry textbook. Above the quotation was the name Gerald Tarkington Smith.

Tark Smith was a square. Most of his classmates at City College knew he was a square. And, I suppose Tark knew it too.

During four years at City College he never went to a booze blast; he didn't even smoke tobacco, to say nothing of pot. I doubt if he knew the names of the first eleven players in the school's Football Hall of Fame. But the thing that really pegged Tark as a king-size drip was his attitude about the plain and fancy cheating that went on all around him.

Not only did Tark refuse to cheat but—well, let's reconstruct a snatch of conversation between Charlie and Jim — no squares, these boys!

"Charles, m'boy, we have really fixed Tark's chariot."

"We have?"

"Charlie, I imagine even you are aware that we're taking a final tomorrow afternoon from old Mossy."

"Yeah, but what does that do to Tark that it doesn't do twice as much to us?"

"See these papers? I had 'em mimeographed. Here's your copy, compliments of the house."

"What are they?"

"Nothing 'much, merely an exact duplicate of the final dear old Middleton Marion Moss is gonna spring on us."

"No!"

"Yeah, and what's more, everybody's gonna have a copy, that is, everybody but Tarkie boy."

"You mean . . ."

"I mean! Tark's gonna find out honesty is the worst policy. He won't even rate a conditional. Got a few more copies to pass out. See you in class, scholar."

And that's the way it was. But it seems there were others who took a dim view of cheating. And somehow copies of the mimeographed sheets found their way back to Old Mossy.

Came the day, as they say. Dr. Middleton Marion Moss gave the final, the roughest, toughest exam in the history of City College. So what happened? Well, Charlie and Jim decided to drop chemistry. And Gerald Tarkington Smith? Well, he managed to squeak by with a C plus — the highest grade made.

Old Mossy asked Tark if he would like to assist him the following year. It all happened a long time ago. Mossy retired last year. There's a new department head now — that square, Tark Smith. Charlie and Jim? I lost track of them after they dropped out of school.

How did I get the story? Firsthand. You see, Tark was my roommate.

Complainers and Doers

You've heard of the
    celebrated Misery Moggs
Who made his living
    in the bogs
Where he caught frogs;
    As a sideline
He sawed logs.
    And through it all
He constantly opined
    The world was going
To the dogs.

Old Terry Singer was not a frog-catcher and he did not saw logs but he really played that tune about the world going to the dogs. Not that he was too far off, mind you, but with all his complaining he never once offered a solution for any of the problems that burdened his conversation. Surely we are all obligated to do more than complain.

I was riding along the highway with Terry the other day and he was lamenting a nationwide problem, one that our town has not been able to avoid. "Bottles and cans," Terry growled, "it looks as though people would have more pride in themselves and in their community." I had to admit he had something but Jim Hoover, who was riding with us, had something to offer.

"I can take care of that," Jim said. And he did. I'm sure you've seen those small tractors at driving ranges. They scoot over the grass and pick up golf balls by the hundreds. In minutes they do a job that would take hours if the balls were picked up by hand. Anyway, at their next meeting Jim talked the councilmen into a contract calling for use of a modified golf ball picker to keep tidy all the roadsides within the city limits. I admire men like Jim.

Like almost everybody else, I catch myself playing Mr. Moggs' role on occasion. Then I think of Jim Hoover. There are two kinds of people in the world, the complainers and the doers. What a tremendous difference in their outlook!

In the Epistle of James, often called the New Testament Book of Proverbs, we read: "But be ye doers of the word, and not hearers only, deluding your own selves. For if any one is a hearer of the word and not a doer, he is like unto a man beholding his natural face in a mirror: for he beholdeth himself, and goeth away, and straightway forgetteth what manner of man he was" (James 1:22-24).

It is interesting to note that the inspired writer, continuing his treatise on "doers of the word" has this to say: "He that looketh into the perfect law, the law of liberty, and so continueth, being not a hearer that forgetteth but a doer that worketh, this man shall be blessed in his doing" (James 1:25).

The Old Man

At first I failed to recognize the old man. His clothes flapped loosely about him as he walked waveringly up the street. Then recognition came — with a shock. When I was a little boy, this man had been my idol. I quickened my pace and caught up with him. We talked about my work in the big city and the many years that had passed. Even so, it was hard to believe this was the man whose ramrod posture, piercing gaze, and basso profundo voice thrilled and chilled worshipers in years gone by. His once rumbling bass was now a weak, squeaky treble.

I remembered lines from Shakespeare's seven ages of man: "With spectacles on nose and pouch on side; His youthful hose, well saved, a world too wide for his shrunk shank; and his big manly voice, turning again to childish treble . . ."

As we chatted it came to me that the old man was confused. He knew me, and yet he did not. Try as he would, he was unable to fit all the pieces together. It was pathetic, but not wholly so.

Here was a man who had lived a full life in the service of God. The ravages of age could not remove his long-established habits of gentility and good breeding. My wife walked up and when he saw her he doffed his hat and bowed in the courtly manner of a bygone day.

The old man's departure from this earth is imminent, yet death holds no terrors for him. His old body is a prison for a youthful spirit that will never die. The apostle Paul must have been thinking along this line when he wrote, "For to me to live is Christ, and to die is gain" (Phil. 1:21).

Paul's great valedictory is a fitting commentary on the life of this old saint too as he nears the end of the road. ". . . The time of my departure is at hand. I have fought a good fight, I have finished my course, I have kept the faith: henceforth there is laid up for me a crown of righteousness, which the Lord, the righteous judge, shall give to me at that day: and not to me only, but also to all them also that love his appearing" (II Tim. 4:6-8, *KJV*).

Thorn in the Flesh

We all have aches and pains and special worries that we could trot out on display from time to time. Fortunately, the average person refrains, most of the time, from telling his woes.

A preacher I know once remarked that he attended more organ recitals than anybody he knew: organs such as eyes, ears, heart, etc. It seems people complain of their ailments to preachers more than they do to their doctors.

John is a good friend of mine and I didn't have the heart to tell him that he was known to his associates as Calamity John. He was constantly singing the blues. It got so bad that even when he felt fine he moaned because he was sure it wouldn't last. And then calamity, or what appeared to be a real calamity, hit John. An old football injury began acting up. There were times when John could hardly walk. John was a salesman and he just had to get around!

Well, you can imagine how Calamity John howled. Every day he became progressively worse. Then one Saturday night I noticed my preacher's sermon subject listed in the paper, "A Thorn in the Flesh." That, I thought, is made to order for Calamity John.

It took some doing but the next morning I had him in church. The first part of the sermon went something like this:

"There are some things for which there is no definite answer or solution. In such instances it is essential that we accept with grace that which cannot be avoided. A case in point is that of the apostle Paul. Paul said, '. . . there was given to me a thorn in the flesh, the messenger of Satan to buffet me, lest I should be exalted above measure. For this thing I besought the Lord thrice, that it might depart from me. And he said unto me, My grace is sufficient for thee.'

"This," the preacher said, "is the echo of our Savior's request in Gethsemane — 'If it be possible!' Remember, if our suffering is inevitable our only course is to accept our lot with continued faith in our heavenly Father's mercy."

Then the preacher quoted those great lines, "God grant me the serenity to accept the things I cannot change; the courage to change the things I can; and the wisdom to know the difference."

After the service John looked at me and grinned. "You tricked me," he said, "but I can take it. You won't hear any more out of me." And I haven't. Nor has anyone else.

It takes a real man to recognize his major fault — and then to do something about it.

Inspiration

"Office Upstairs"

Old Doc Raleigh was buried last week. Just about everybody in town attended the funeral, and for awhile it looked as though everybody in town would deliver a speech. I'm sure Old Doc wouldn't have approved of all those eulogies. Doc was the kind of man who always had time to do a good deed, but he never had time to listen to words of thanks.

I was reminded of a story I read when I was a boy. There was a kindly country doctor, a general practitioner. After serving the community unselfishly for about forty years, Dr. Raleigh was found one morning at his desk in his upstairs office. Mrs. Brown, the cleaning woman, thought he was asleep. She often found him that way. He was asleep all right, his last sleep.

The townspeople got together after the funeral and talked about a fitting memorial for the man who had ministered to them so faithfully over the years. The librarian suggested a special reference room in his honor. The president of the school board suggested the new gym be named for him. The mayor was in favor of calling the new wayside picnic grounds "Raleigh Park." And so it went. But they couldn't reach a decision.

Finally, the caretaker of the city cemetery stood up and said, "I know a fittin' memorial for old Doc Raleigh."

There was an amused look on the chairman's face as he said, "You do? Well, Tom, let's have it."

"Just take his sign down," said the caretaker, "and put it over his grave."

There was dead silence for a minute or two and then a murmur of approval began to run through the room. Jim Stokes got to his feet and said, "I make a motion we put Doc's sign over his grave."

The motion carried. They did just that. The sign read:

ROBERT RALEIGH, M.D.
OFFICE UPSTAIRS

Words to Live By

Now and then statements are made that fit a situation or condition with absolute perfection. I was reading one of Elton Trueblood's books recently when just such a statement seemed to leap at me from the page. "Words like 'take up your cross daily' seem quaint to a generation which is only mildly shocked by the advertisement of the solid gold putter."

This, of all times past and perhaps all times future, is THE outstanding age of affluence. The farmer drives an air-conditioned tractor and has his lunch in his air-conditioned home, a lunch prepared in an all-electric kitchen.

This same farmer, as well as his city cousin, drives his air-conditioned car to church and listens in air-conditioned comfort to a stream-lined sermon which, more often than not, has little light and is noticeably lacking in heat.

Religion, to many, is nothing to get excited about. Like modern wearing apparel, religion has become casual and, in some cases, slovenly. But God does not accept such religion.

These passages indicate the urgency of the religion of Christ: ". . . Present your bodies as a living sacrifice, holy, acceptable to God, which is your spiritual worship" (Rom. 12:1). "It seemed good unto us . . . to choose men and send them . . . with . . . Barnabas and Paul, men who have risked their lives for the sake of our Lord Jesus Christ" (Acts 15:25, 26). "Strive to enter by the narrow door; for many, I tell you, will seek to enter, and will not be able" (Luke 13:24). "Preach the word; be urgent in season and out of season; convince, rebuke, and exhort, be unfailing in patience and in teaching" (II Tim. 4:2). ". . . Be faithful unto death, and I will give you the crown of life" (Rev. 2:10).

Finally, look at that towering passage that is so needed by a materialistic society. "Blessed are they that do his commandments, that they may have right to the tree of life, and may enter in through the gates into the city" (Rev. 22:14, *KJV*).

The Fool Hath Said

Dr. H. Carrington Carruthers and Dr. Smith Boldingham are good neighbors. Each has a high regard for the other. For more than twenty years they have referred to each other affectionately as Carry and Boldy. Carry is a scientist. He earned his doctorate at MIT. Boldy holds a Ph.D. from Vanderbilt. Carry teaches at the university and Boldy is the preacher at the big church on Main Street.

Carry has taken many a swipe at Boldy's implicit faith in God as the supreme being, creator, and ruler of the universe. "The Bible account of creation is utterly fantastic, Boldy," Carry would say, or, "Now, Boldy, how can you possibly believe there is a God who rules in the affairs of men? Surely it is more reasonable to believe in the natural order of things. Your trouble, Boldy," he would say with exaggerated patience, "is that you're too superstitious. As a matter of fact, you are just a step removed from the benighted heathen you preachers are so fond of talking about."

One evening Boldy called his friend. "Come over, Carry," he said, "I have something to show you."

When Carry came over Boldy took him out to the workshop. Boldy, who was quite an amateur mechanic, proudly showed his atheist friend an ingenious steam engine. It represented many hours of spare-time work.

"Boldy, it's beautiful," Carry cried, "when did you make it?"

"Make it?" Boldy responded, "I didn't make it; it just happened."

"Quit kidding. When did you make it? How long did it take?"

"I'm not kidding," Boldy replied with a straight face, "I tell you it just happened. When I came out to the shop — there it was, the pieces must have fallen together — just like the universe." And then he asked his friend archly, "You believe me, don't you? It would be fantastic to think that somebody made it. You can't think that, can you?"

When Carry left for home that evening he had a strange look on his face. Ordinarily he was a talkative man but that night his wife couldn't get a word out of him. He was preoccupied, to say the least.

"The heavens declare the glory of God; and the firmament sheweth his handywork" (Ps. 19:1, *KJV*). The psalmist also said, "The fool hath said in his heart, There is no God" (Ps. 14:1).

Sparrows and June Graduates

It was commencement time and I was hurrying across the campus after a rainy, blustery night. A tiny baby bird lay in the path; it had been blown out of its nest. There it lay, dead before it had had a chance to try its wings.

Later that morning as the president of the college was introducing me to the senior class, the analogy hit me — hard! There before me were boys and girls who eagerly awaited an opportunity to try their wings. Would they have that opportunity? Would they grasp it? What effect would the winds of chance have on them? Would they fly or fall? rise above adversity? succumb to affluence? yield to poverty?

My speech had been carefully prepared. It was liberally sprinkled with sage observations and sparkling quotations — which I did not use. I put my prepared speech aside and talked instead about God and His love for mankind.

Young people can be pretty blasé these days. Perhaps their attitude stems from what they see in those who are supposed to be their guides and examples. However, that day they listened. I suppose they sensed my genuine interest in their welfare. Of greater importance, I am sure, they sensed God's love and concern for them.

Long ago Jesus said, "Are not two sparrows sold for a penny? And not one of them shall fall on the ground without your Father's will . . . Fear not, therefore; Ye are of more value than many sparrows" (Matt. 10:29, 31).

Help for Unbelief

There are two kinds of unbelievers in this world. One is the type who goes about shouting his unbelief. He doesn't believe and he isn't satisfied unless everybody around him knows that he doesn't believe. He is fond of saying, "If there is a God, let Him strike me dead!" Then, when no visible evidence of God's wrath is apparent, he looks about triumphantly and says, "See, I told you so."

But what about the other kind of unbelief? We find it in the man who tries to believe and wants to believe but in all honesty and sincerity he just can't seem to find faith.

There is an account in the ninth chapter of Mark of just such a man. This man had a son who was a victim of violent seizures. The father brought the boy to Jesus' disciples but they were unable to help him. We don't know what the man thought about this failure. He may have said, "Well, it's just as I thought; they can't help my boy."

But the disciples brought the boy to Jesus and just as they did so the lad had a violent seizure. Jesus asked the father how long he had been this way. The father told the Master the boy had been in this state ever since he was a child. And then he said, "If thou canst do anything, have compassion on us, and help us."

Jesus said, "If thou canst!" Obviously the man failed to comprehend he was speaking to the One who "was in the beginning with God" and that "without him was not anything made that hath been made."

Then Jesus said, "All things are possible to him that believeth."

When Jesus spoke these words the father said piteously, "I believe; help thou mine unbelief." So here he was — believing yet not believing, wanting to believe yet in need of assistance that he might believe. This man was not interested in hiring a hall and shouting his skepticism to the world. He wanted more than anything to believe, but he was finding it terribly difficult.

Jesus, according to Mark's account, then "rebuked the unclean spirit, saying unto him, Thou dumb and deaf spirit, I command thee, come out of him, and enter no more into him." From that moment the boy was healed.

We don't know what the father said or did after that. We never hear of them again. We would not want to speculate, but it seems plausible to picture this father and son as faithful followers of Christ from that moment on.

When a man wants to believe, it's safe to say he will believe. "Belief cometh of hearing, and hearing by the word of Christ" (Rom. 10:17). Amen.

All Things Are Possible

I don't know who first said "Never underestimate the power of a woman." I do know this: he should have added, "or the power of suggestion." I was driving through Tennessee some time back and stopped in Nashville for lunch. In scanning the paper I saw a story about a famous evangelist who was conducting a meeting in the municipal auditorium. We'll call the evangelist John, simply because that is not his name. John was a schoolmate of mine. Believe me, I knew him when!

In those days John was a hulking, awkward, thick-tongued boy. His prospects as a first-class tackle were excellent but as a preacher — well, hardly.

It took some doing but I managed to contact John by telephone and suggested we get together for a few minutes. He seemed delighted.

When John walked into the restaurant all eyes turned toward him. He was as big as ever, even bigger, but so different from the boy I knew. Now he was graceful in his walk and manner. There was a smile on his face, and it was genuine.

After the usual exchanges and a liberal sprinkling of "and do you remember so and so," I decided to ask him about his career. "John," I said seriously, "if you don't mind my saying so, I didn't expect you to develop into an outstanding evangelist. But for the past few years I've been reading reports of your work and I must say, it's fantastic. Tell me, what's your secret?"

There was no sham about John and he didn't pretend that he was not a nationally known figure. He replied simply, "It isn't my secret; it's my mother's."

"You'll have to explain that one," I said.

John explained. Ever since he could remember his mother introduced him to her friends: "This is John, my little preacher." The idea became so firmly implanted in John's mind that he never really considered any other occupation.

John worked at various jobs during high school and he had a football scholarship in college. Just before graduation he was approached by professional scouts with a juicy contract. But John just smiled and said he already had a job. He was preaching then at a little country place that couldn't afford a regular preacher.

When it was time to leave John said, "And what do you suppose my mother's favorite passage of Scripture was?" Without pausing for a reply he quoted musingly, "All things are possible to him that believeth."

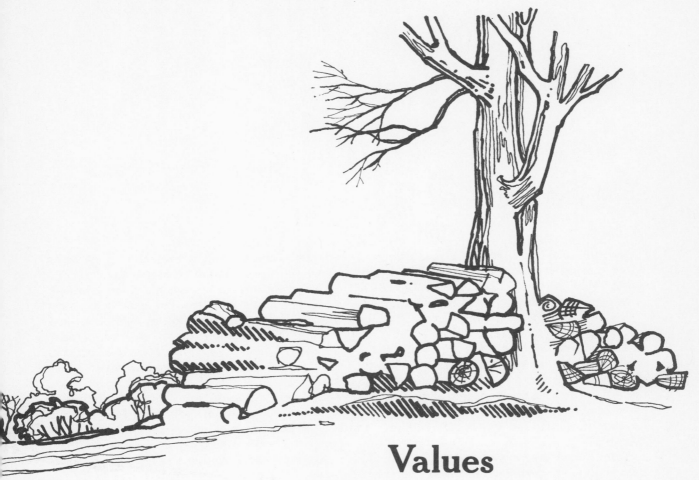

Values

The Glory of God

Did you see this cartoon: A man was pictured looking at vacation folders. He asks his wife, "How would you like to take a trip around the world this year?" and she replies, "No, dear, let's go somewhere else." It's too painfully accurate to be really funny.

This matter of being fed up with things, surfeited with a superabundance of everything and left with a feeling of ennui, is typical of large segments of our society. There is a need to recapture that wonderful virtue of little children, the ability to look and to wonder.

Think about the wonder which engulfed the two young Japanese who discovered the enormous Ikeya-Seki Comet, using only homemade telescopes.

About that time one of my friends wrote: "I was flying down to Florida on an early morning flight. I knew I would be in good position to see the comet along about daylight so I sat on the left side of the southbound plane. And just before daybreak I saw it. Its immensity thrilled me, and I'm not even an amateur astronomer. But the thought of that gigantic object, with a tail millions of miles long, hurtling through space at such incredible speed — well, believe me, I was thrilled. As the sun brightened the east, the comet began to fade. I pulled out my Bible and read again those ancient words of the psalmist, 'The heavens declare the glory of God; and the firmament sheweth his handywork. Day unto day uttereth speech, And night unto night sheweth knowledge. There is no speech nor language; where their voice is not heard. Their line is gone out through all the earth, and their words to the end of the world.' I closed my Bible and sat staring out the window.

The stewardess pulled me out of my reverie. 'See anything interesting out there?' she asked. She looked a little puzzled when I replied, 'Yes, the glory of almighty God!' "

The same psalmist also said, "O Jehovah, our Lord, How excellent is thy name in all the earth. . . . When I consider thy heavens the work of thy fingers, The moon and the stars, which thou hast ordained; What is man, that thou art mindful of him?"

The Measure of a Man

The true measure of a man is an elusive thing. Sometimes, however, the real man emerges in words which he knows are to be his last.

There was the day, for example, when General Douglas MacArthur gave his farewell address to the cadets at West Point. He knew his days were numbered when he said, "The shadows are lengthening for me. The twilight is here. My days of old have vanished — tone and tints. They have gone glimmering through the dreams of things that were. Their memory is one of wondrous beauty, watered by tears and coaxed and caressed by the smiles of yesterday (and) . . . always there echoes and re-echoes: Duty, honor, country."

In a time when duty, honor and country are given scant attention by all too many and when riot and insurrection appear to be the order of the day, it is well to consider a great man's devotion.

Douglas MacArthur was a great man and a great soldier. An even greater man and greater soldier is seen in the person of the apostle Paul. He too delivered a farewell address. It is found in a short letter addressed to a young man named Timothy. Its message, however, is applicable to Christian soldiers in all ages and for all time to come: "Always be steady, endure suffering, do the work of an evangelist, fulfil your ministry. For I am already being offered, on the point of being sacrificed; and the time of my departure has come. I have fought the good fight, I have finished the race, I have kept the faith. Henceforth there is laid up for me the crown of righteousness, which the Lord, the righteous judge, will award to me on that Day, and not only to me, but also to all them that have loved his appearing" (II Tim. 4:5-8).

Attitudes

There's a beautiful waterfall in the foothills of the Cumberlands. Perhaps you've seen it; it's reputed to be the highest falls east of the Rockies. It used to be a pretty wild and rugged place. Nowadays, however, anybody can drive to the summit in his car.

A friend of mine, old Lew Daniel, took his boys on a camping trip up there last summer. They could have driven to the top but Lew's boys would have none of that. They wanted to hike.

"And away we go," one of them yelled, and off they went, with Lew huffing and puffing in the rear. About halfway up, with the boys whooping and hollering in the distance, Lew twisted his ankle. There was a break in the trees and Lew's misfortune could be viewed by the more prudent souls who had chosen to walk up the smooth road.

Well, after awhile a fellow came sauntering by. "Hi!" he called to Lew. And then, seeing Lew's contorted face, he asked, "Anything wrong?"

"Sprained my ankle," Lew moaned.

"Too bad," the man murmured as he walked on.

About ten minutes later, while Lew was struggling to get his shoe off (his ankle was begining to swell rapidly now), another man ambled by. He took in Lew's predicament at a glance and observed piously, "These mountain trails can be treacherous." Then he walked on.

About a half hour and many moans and groans later the boys came scampering back looking for their dad. At the same time a third man spotted Lew. After a short conversation he said authoritatively, "Stay with your dad, boys; I'll go back to camp and get my car. From the looks of that foot your dad's going to need some medical attention." And to Lew he said, "Take it easy, old man; I'll be right back."

And the boys did and Lew did and the stranger did.

There's a story told by Jesus that deals with three men and their attitudes toward an unfortunate fellowman. I heartily recommend that you read it. It begins with the twenty-fifth verse of the tenth chapter of the Gospel according to Luke.

Good Intentions

When children praise their parents we feel it is a triumph of parental rearing and a milestone in the lives of the children. However, there are times when childish praise has a dubious ring. For instance, there was the boy who said his dad only got as far as the fifth grade but he was just as smart as if he had finished the sixth.

This brings us to the matter of intent. We are all aware of the aphorism about the road to a certain ill-favored destination being paved with good intentions. There are ever so many illustrations in the Bible as well as in our own lives as to the futility of intentions when they are not backed by action.

The letter we should have written yesterday and can't get to today is to be written tomorrow — maybe. The disparity and danger regarding intent and performance is this: If we allow little, unimportant things to pile up there will come a time when big, extremely important things will receive the same treatment.

Take the case of a fellow named Felix. He was listening to some mighty good preaching. The preacher's name was Paul and his subject was "righteousness, self-control, and the judgment to come." Strong medicine! The evil governor was terrified. When Paul got around to talking about judgment to come, Felix had good reason to be frightened.

The governor's fear was a healthy sign. It's good to be scared when we find ourselves doing what we know is wrong. But then Felix ruined it all. He said, "Go thy way for this time; and when I have a convenient season, I will call for thee" (Acts 24:25, *KJV*). So far as we know, that convenient season never came.

Is it your intention to do something that would please your mother or father, your sister or brother, your son or daughter, your employer or employee? By all means do it now. Is it your intention to live in accordance with the commands and principles of the Lord Jesus Christ? Well, then, how about putting those good intentions into practice —

NOW!

You're the Greatest

"Pop, you're the greatest!" These words came back to Stan over and over, day after day — after his boy Mickey had been tried and found guilty of grand larceny. Mickey and his buddies had stolen enough goods to equip a first-class store.

Whatever caused Mickey to think it was all right to steal? Stan had turned the problem over in his mind a thousand times. Now he knew the answer. His wife, Emma, knew the answer too. As yet, though, neither had the courage to admit the truth.

Stan remembered the times he had boasted to Mickey about shortchanging braceros who had crossed the border to work the harvest fields. They were unable to speak English. It was easy. Emma remembered the time she had told Mickey to tell the paper boy to come back for his money the following week; she knew they would be moving the next day.

Finally, Stan and Emma admitted their wrongs to each other. That was a tremendous step; it led them to get down on their knees and confess to God. After that Stan wrote:

"Dear Mickey, Your mother and I have asked ourselves what went wrong, why you got into such a mess, and why you are now serving time in prison. Well, Mickey, we have the answer. I guess we have known all along. You thought I was really great when I lied and cheated. You thought Mom was pretty slick when she avoided paying that poor little kid what she owed him for the newspaper. What we want to say, Mickey, is that we are the ones who should be in prison. You have done exactly as you were taught to do — by our example. We would give everything we have if we could undo the wrong we have done. Maybe it isn't too late. When you get out we'll start all over. Believe me, son, we will!"

Example is one of the most powerful of all influences — for good or evil. In the Book of First Kings it is said of Jeroboam, one of the most wicked men who ever lived, that "he walked in all the sins of his father, which he had done before him."

Righteous Indignation

Joe Phillips is a rough-hewn individualist. Folks are proud of Joe. They say there's nobody quite like him, and then they usually add, "we're thankful for that." But the way they grin indicates they don't mean it.

Joe made one of his infrequent trips to the big city some weeks ago. He finished his business and decided to walk to his hotel—through the park. Apparently Joe didn't know that city parks are jungles — after dark that is.

Three or four thugs decided to give Joe a going over. And Joe, a brute of a man, gave them a going over instead. When the police arrived, Joe helped load the thugs into the wagon — and then he climbed in. Later he tagged along when two of the boys were taken to the hospital. He paid the bill when the boys were released.

The next time Joe came to town he met the policeman who had carted the boys to the calaboose. The policeman questioned Joe about the interest he had taken in "some worthless rascals who might have killed" him.

Joe's answer stayed with the cop. It has stayed with me. I hope it will stay with you: "Avenge not yourselves, beloved, but give place unto the wrath of God: for it is written, Vengeance belongeth unto me: I will recompense, saith the Lord" (Rom. 12:19).

There is another statement from the Book of books that we would do well to remember: "Be not overcome of evil, but overcome evil with good" (Rom. 12:21).

Reflections

"Where There Is No Vision"

Windy Walker is president of one of the service clubs in our town. He heads a group called the Civic Boosters and he is chairman of the City Beautiful Campaign. He is also a member of the school board.

There was a knot of people on the corner and Windy was doing the talking. In fact, there is seldom a time when Windy isn't talking. He was in an expansive mood. He exuded patriotism as he launched into a monologue on the virtues of the American system of education. He wound up his discourse by unloosing a tirade against "Godless Russia."

Sam Chapman was suffering in silence during Windy's speech and when Windy stopped to catch his breath Sam asked, "Windy, you are a member of the school board aren't you?"

"Yes, I am," Windy responded, and then he began to rehash his wearisome speech.

Sam cut in, "Windy, do you know that the Soviet Union and America are the only two countries in the world, that is, among the advanced people of the world, whose educational systems are completely separated from religion?"

Windy's mouth popped open but no sound was heard. Finally he sputtered indignantly, "What do you mean? Are you trying to tell us that our educational system is no better than the Russians?"

"No, Windy," Sam said, "I simply asked if you were aware of the striking similarity. The Soviet Union and the United States of America are the only two countries in the world that are attempting to operate their educational systems without religion. And so," Sam continued, "if you are going to expose us to your pep talks on the greatness of our system I, for one, want to know how relegating God and the religion of the Lord Jesus Christ to limbo has improved the spiritual and moral outlook of our nation."

Windy voiced a few platitudes but he really had nothing to say. And this exchange set me to thinking. It is high time for thoughtful people throughout our nation to express themselves. Surely the framers of the Constitution had no intention of abandoning that priceless heritage we call religion. Yet each year our society becomes more secularistic. Each year education and government move farther away from religion.

"Where there is no vision," the ancient prophet warned, "the people cast off restraint . . ." (Prov. 29:18). In a time and in a land where just about anything goes, the words *vision* and *restraint* have little meaning. A knowledge of God and of our Savior, as revealed in the Bible, gives meaning, as well as life and relevance, to these words.

The Fishermen

Emmet Dean was, as he put it, "a nature guy." He loved the outdoors, the warm sun of summer and the cold blast of winter, running brooks and frozen lakes, forests of green and white winter wonderland — all of nature was unceasingly wonderful to Emmet. This was his religion. ". . . tongues in trees, books in the running brooks, sermons in stones, and good in everything."

As for conventional religion, with all its duties and responsibilities, Emmet was fond of saying "I don't believe in formal religion, churches, preachers, sermons, hymn singing, and praying; I think all that stuff is the bunk." When he warmed up to his subject he was especially fond of saying: "I think religion is a racket." And occasionally he would ask, "What good are churches except to take up a man's time and relieve him of his money?"

As a captive audience of one, on a long fishing trip, Frank Sawyer took all he could of this sort of negativism. Finally, he put his rod and reel down and said: "Turn around, Emmet; it's my turn to talk. First, I want to say that your callous attitude amazes me. And since you are so belligerent, I'm going to let you have it straight. "I'm a Christian, Emmet. As a Christian I believe in God, in Jesus Christ His Son, in the Holy Spirit, and in the Bible as His revealed will."

Emmet tried to interrupt but Frank said, "You've had your say, Emmet; now it's my turn. Look at it this way: If the church is really meaningless, a racket as you say, then Christ's death was the world's greatest extravagance. Why do you suppose God gave His Son if His body, the church, isn't important? The writer of Proverbs said, 'He that trusteth in his own heart is a fool.' And during one of the worst periods of Israel's history the inspired historian recorded the fact that 'every man did that which was right in his own eyes.' Emmet, we played ball together all through school, and we played by the rules. What you need to do is to start playing the game of life by God's rules."

Jesus once asked a simple question, a question based on a profound principle. Here it is, according to Phillips' translation: "What is the point of calling me, 'Lord, Lord,' without doing what I tell you to do?"

Our Lord's question requires an answer.

Sound Speech

Robinson Crusoe was written by Daniel De-Foe in 1719 and has continued to be a perennial favorite ever since. DeFoe's novel was based on the actual experience of Alexander Selkirk who, after quarreling with his captain, was put ashore on an island in the South Seas.

Selkirk wrote the lines, "I am monarch of all I survey. My right there is none to dispute." Yet when Selkirk was rescued from his lonely strand, after four years of complete isolation, his rescuers could scarcely understand him. For want of use he had almost forgotten his own language.

There is little likelihood of our being marooned on a lonely island in the manner of Alexander Selkirk. And there is little chance of our ever losing the power of speech because there is no one with whom we may carry on a conversation. However, there is constant danger of misusing the wonderful gift of speech.

The Bible has much to say about right and wrong usages of speech, not in the areas of enunciation, pronunciation, or grammar, but rather the matter of including godliness and excluding all devilishness from our speech.

In writing to the Colossians the apostle Paul exhorted, "Let your speech be always with grace, seasoned with salt, that ye may know how ye ought to answer every man" (Col. 4:6).

It was James who said, "If any stumbleth not in word, the same is a perfect man, able to bridle the whole body" (James 3:2).

Much of the world's woe has come about because of harsh speech on the part of unfeeling men and women. In his letter to Titus the apostle Paul enlarges upon this theme: "Young men likewise exhort to be sober minded." he said, "in all things showing thyself a pattern of good works: in doctrine showing uncorruptness, gravity, sincerity, sound speech, that cannot be condemned; that he that is of the contrary part may be ashamed, having no evil thing to say of you" (Titus 2:6-8).

A Still Small Voice

Most of us are like Terry Templeton who, up until the time of his accident, thought those warning signs "Slow down and live," were designed solely for others.

Terry was noted for his loud voice and heavy foot. And one day the law of averages caught up with him. He was breezing along at about eighty-five when he came to the one-way bridge warning. It was ironic that a "Slow down and live" sign was the last thing he saw before he went through the bridge rail.

During Terry's long convalescence he became a regular Bible reader. This loud, brash fellow became quiet and thoughtful. When the preacher came by to see him, Terry was content to lie back and listen. This was astonishing because, to put it mildly, Terry had never been a good listener.

The preacher was puzzled, too, for awhile. But after he had visited Terry several times it all came out. Before his accident Terry had been putting on an act. He thought he had to be loud in order to be heard and appreciated. He monopolized conversations to prove his leadership ability. He drove like a mad man to impress people with his nerve.

If Terry thought of God at all, it is more than likely that he thought of him in terms of howling winds, rolling thunder, and flashing lightning.

Late one night Terry made a startling discovery. When the preacher came to see him the following day Terry said, "I found out something last night." He paused a moment and then he said earnestly, "If I ever get out of here, my life is going to be different."

The preacher sat quietly as Terry picked up the Bible and began to read the familiar lines, "Jehovah passed by, and a great and strong wind rent the mountains, and broke in pieces the rocks before Jehovah; but Jehovah was not in the wind: and after the wind an earthquake; but Jehovah was not in the earthquake: and after the earthquake a still small voice" (I Kings 19:11, 12).

Terry closed the book. The preacher asked softly, "And what did you find out?"

"I found," Terry replied, "that the voice of God is in His word, the Bible. It's a still small voice, but a mighty voice, and it fills the entire earth."

The Book

Tenure is a guarantee of sorts that a college teacher cannot be fired. A major requirement for tenure is the publishing of books.

George Joseph Johnson is a teacher in a well-known university. He has several highly technical books to his credit and his tenure is pretty well assured. But George is something more than a university professor and more than a successful writer; he is a dedicated Christian.

George and several of his colleagues were engaged in a rather warm discussion about noted authors and great books when he asked, "Have you ever heard the account of Scott's estimate of the Bible?"

It seems they had not heard the story so George proceeded to relate it. "When Walter Scott was on his deathbed, he called for 'the book.' Scott's nephew was puzzled, knowing Scott had written so many books, and he asked, 'Which book?' The dying man replied, 'There is but one book, the Bible.' "

"Oh, come now, George," one of his fellow teachers said with some annoyance in his voice, "you surely don't swallow that!"

In reply George pulled out his Bible and began to read in his rich baritone voice, "Seek ye out of the book of the Lord and read." "The grass withereth, the flower fadeth: but the word of our God shall stand forever." "The law of the Lord is perfect, converting the soul: the testimony of the Lord is sure, making wise the simple. The statutes of the Lord are right, rejoicing the heart: the commandment of the Lord is pure, enlightening the eyes. The fear of the Lord is clean, enduring forever: the judgments of the Lord are true and righteous altogether."

George read several more passages from the Old Testament. Then, turning to the New Testament, he read, "Heaven and earth shall pass away, but my words shall not pass away."

George's colleagues looked thoughtful as the bell rang and the session broke up. I know. I was there.

Pushover

Janie Simmons was a writer. She had worked with the local television station for several years and could dash off copy with the greatest of ease. She was also an accomplished singer. Janie was also a CPA. But above all, Janie was, and is, a Christian.

When Janie left town to begin a new job in New York, she was assigned to work on an account with Charlie Fowler. Charlie's gaze roamed up and down as Janie approached his desk. He grinned appreciatively and decided then and there that this little girl would be a pushover.

Charlie came in early the next morning and found Janie alone in her office. She was reading. "Whatcha reading?" Charlie asked, naming a racy magazine.

"Oh, no," Janie said, "I'm reading something much more interesting."

"No kidding," Charlie responded, with a notable lack of originality, "well, what are you reading?"

"It's a personal letter."

"What's the writer's name?"

"His name is John. And it isn't really a personal letter."

Charlie was puzzled but he pressed on, "Well, who is it addressed to?"

"Why, to Christians everywhere," Janie said as she placed a small New Testament on her desk. "You see, I was reading the first general epistle of John."

Charlie looked dumfounded, and looks were not deceiving. " 'Scuse me, Janie," he mumbled as he walked off.

How did I hear about Janie and Charlie? Charlie told me about the incident himself. He told me about it while we were waiting for Mrs. Charlie Fowler (Janie) to meet us for lunch. I was in New York for a brief visit and had called the agency that morning. Janie didn't keep us waiting long. She looked prettier than ever. As for Charlie, it was obvious that he adored his lovely bride. We had an excellent lunch, much good talk, and all too soon it was time to go.

Caring

Man's Greatest Need

There's an old story of a student in a far-away place in the Orient who was walking down a lane with his teacher. The young man said, "Teacher, I want to learn."

At that moment they came to a stream of water. Without a word the teacher plunged the young man under the water and held him there. In a moment the teacher released his pupil and asked, "When you were under water, what did you want most?"

"Air! Master," the young man gasped.

"So," the teacher said, "if you would learn, you must desire learning — as much as you wanted air while you were under the water."

In our materialistic world so many people feel their lives would be complete if they could have all the necessities: air, water, food, and sleep — plus a liberal supply of luxuries such as a house with central heating, one or two air conditioned automobiles, plenty of money, paid vacations, and unlimited recreation with large amounts of leisure time.

The problem with the wonderful, material blessings all about us is that they don't last and they don't meet a man's spiritual needs. Even the man who "has everything" doesn't have it very long. James asks, "What is your life?" And then he supplies the answer to his own question: "Ye are a vapor that appeareth for a little time, and then vanisheth away."

One day a delegation of Greeks came to Philip with a request. They said, "Sir, we would see Jesus." And this is the heart of the matter. Jesus, the Son of God, the Savior of mankind, is what men need most. Long ago Jesus said, "I am come that ye may have life and have it more abundantly."

A wealthy man once informed his preacher proudly and confidently that in ten years he would be a millionaire. The preacher asked quietly, "And what will you do with it a hundred years from now?"

We do need air, water, food, sleep, and recreation, but our real and lasting need is Jesus.

Too Near Where I Got In

Lee Watkins has been in politics for more years than he would probably care to admit. He began his career as a state representative. Some years later he made a successful bid for governor. Then he ran for senator and was swept into office by an overwhelming majority. He could have written a book entitled, "How To Be Successful in Politics Without Really Trying."

Lee knows the ropes in Washington and he has a knack for saying and doing the right things among his constituents. Take, for example, the matter of religion. In his campaign speeches Lee manages to let people know that he became a member of the church when he was a young man and that he has been an active member ever since. What he doesn't mention is the real truth of the matter, namely, that he has never worked at his religion.

Lee's son, daughter-in-law, and grandson were visiting recently. Lee III is quite a boy, smart as a whip and, according to Lee, he looks just like his grandfather.

It must have been two o'clock in the morning when the household was awakened by a resounding thump. Lee jumped up and ran into his grandson's room. There was the boy, lying flat on the floor and looking rather sheepish. "How did you happen to fall out of bed?" Lee asked.

"I don't know, Grampy," the youngster replied, "unless maybe I went to sleep too near where I got in."

Some time later Lee went to church in his home town. The preacher talked about the futility of religion when one's religion is in name only. "The reason it is so easy for people to be satisfied with less than their best," he said, "is because they never venture very far into the church."

Little Lee's words came back to the senator. "I don't know, Grampy, unless I went to sleep too near where I got in."

How far had he ventured into the church? What had he contributed to its growth? Was he responsible for leading anyone to the Lord? These were the disturbing questions with which the senator wrestled as he returned to Washington. "Lee Watkins," he said to himself, "with all your hectic activity you've been asleep on the greatest job of all."

"Awake, thou that sleepest, and arise from the dead, and Christ shall shine upon thee" (Eph. 5:14, *KJV*).

Accentuate the Positive

J. E. B. Jones, Jeb for short, is a mild-mannered man whose rich, baritone voice is rather startling, coming from such a frail-looking body. And Jeb, a successful businessman, executive, and member of a number of important boards, has another feature that's even stronger than his superb voice. I'm talking about his positive approach to life.

For instance, last week there was a heated discussion at the school board meeting about a replacement for James Anders Pursley, the retiring president of the little college of which our town is so proud. It's a four-year college now and fully accredited. Dr. Pursley is stepping down because, as he put it, old age finally caught up with him.

Everybody knew it would take some doing to replace a man like Pursley. And Jim Smith, a member of the board, said he knew just the man. Jim went into a long account of the obvious, including the state of the world in general and our town in particular. He included a tirade on juvenile delinquency and wound up by submitting the name of a well-known man who, he said, was against every form of wrong doing. "In fact," Jim said stoutly, "everybody knows how he fights against everything that's wrong." Then he went on to list the various evils his man was against.

At this point Jeb asked in his deep, probing voice, "That's fine, Jim, but what is he for?"

"What is he for?" Jim spluttered. "Why, I'm sure he's for a lot of things."

"I was reading somewhere the other day," Jeb went on in his imperturbable manner, "about the epitaph of Cato the censor of ancient Rome. It says, 'He loved not right half so much as he hated wrong.' That epitaph is neither impressive nor complimentary. Gentlemen," Jeb continued, turning to the other members of the board, "any negativism in our next president should be a by-product of his positivism. If he's *for* the right things you can mark it down, he'll be *against* the wrong things."

A long time ago the apostle Paul urged, Let us "be ready unto every good work." Our nation has reached a point where it has become absolutely essential that we accentuate the positive.

Tough and Fair

Miss Mary Bainton Browning, tall, spare, grim-visaged, was well known by the greater part of the townspeople as the stern disciplinarian of the seventh grade. Many of her former pupils, now grown and with children of their own, are not likely to forget Miss Mary's unbending insistence on strong disciplinary measures. They also remember that she was as fair as she was stern.

"Walter, I said there was to be no talking," intoned Mary Bainton Browning in her dreaded "assignment" voice. "Bring me, as your special assignment, a one-thousand-word essay on the subject of 'obedience' — tomorrow morning without fail."

"But Miss Browning . . ."

"Don't explain," said Miss Browning firmly, "just be sure you have the completed assignment tomorrow morning."

Walter was a quiet little boy. He was cheerful, inventive, and not given to mischievousness — at least not to the extent of some of the boys who were constantly on the lookout for ways and means of side-stepping the rules. Miss Browning watched Walter as he left the classroom. She noted a suspicion of a tear in his eye. "Well," she said to herself, "I can't afford to let the bars down, not at this stage of the game."

The following morning Walter handed in his essay. Miss Browning accepted it without a word. Later, in study hall, she read it through. Then she read it again.

"Teachers know almost eveything, but not quite," Walter's essay began, "and even the best of teachers can make mistakes." From that point on the little fellow carefully explained that he had found a nickel on the floor, had raised his hand to ask permission to speak, thought he saw Miss Browning nod her head in assent (his glasses were broken and he couldn't see clearly), and only then did he ask his desk-mate if he had lost the nickel.

"Children," Miss Browning said at the beginning of the next class, "I have an essay I want to read to you."

That's why folks in Centertown love Miss Browning. Stern? Oh, yes, but she is also fair. Solomon said a long time ago, "A wise man will hear, and will increase learning" (Prov. 1:5).

Why Must These Things Happen?

Every man, at some time or other, finds himself asking why things happen as they do. Floods and fires, earthquakes and tornados, wars and pestilence. Why? Or that sweet little girl whose father accidentally ran over her and killed her in the driveway of her own home. Why? Financial reverses, a bright young college student, lost to dope, a young mother, horribly mutilated in a senseless mugging — why?

These are some of life's imponderables. There are some questions that have no answer in this world. Far back in the Book of Deuteronomy is this arresting statement, "The secret things belong unto the Lord our God: but those things which are revealed belong unto us and to our children forever . . ." (Deut. 29:29).

Long ago the Lord turned the question back to his servant Job when He asked, "Have the gates of death been opened unto thee? or hast thou seen the doors of the shadow of death?" (Job 38:17).

Mankind has been asking "why?" since the beginning of time. Even Jesus, in that memorable scene on Golgotha, asked the poignant question, "My God, my God, why hast thou forsaken me?" The Christian must look beyond the horror and dread of the moment to the goodness of God in all of time. It is imperative that questions regarding God's motives be shunted aside. The best way to do this is to begin ministering to the ills of those who are suffering all about us. Where to begin? Begin next door, on the adjoining farm, in the same apartment building, or in our own home.

Here is the testimony of the beloved apostle John: "We have known and believed the love that God hath to us. God is love; and he that dwelleth in love dwelleth in God, and God in him. Herein is our love made perfect, that we may have boldness in the day of judgment: because as he is, so are we in this world. There is no fear in love; but perfect love casteth out fear: because fear hath torment. He that feareth is not made perfect in love. We love him, because he first loved us. If a man say, I love God, and hateth his brother, he is a liar: for he that loveth not his brother whom he hath seen, how can he love God whom he hath not seen? And this commandment have we from him, That he who loveth God love his brother also" (I John 4:16-21).

We help ourselves most when we help others. Paul said it; let us believe it: "If any man's work abide which he hath built thereupon, he shall receive a reward" (I Cor. 3:14).

Music Hath Charms

It is good to get off to ourselves now and then. Even our Savior found it necessary to get off to Himself at times. You recall the apostle John tells of Jesus going into a mountain alone. So no matter how gregarious a man may be, there are times when he needs to get to himself — to think, to meditate, and to take inventory.

But when a man wants to be alone all the time and when he is completely antisocial, we wonder about him. Take Sam Carter, for example. Samuel Carter, Ph.D., lived alone, worked alone, cooked his own meals, and if he did any talking at all, it was to himself. Silent Sam. That's what the town folks called him. Dr. Carter wasn't always that way, he began living the life of a recluse following the death of his wife. "Too bad," people would say, "but what can you do with a man like that?"

Well, something was done. It pulled Sam right out of his shell. Susan Richards, who was a teacher at the college, passed by Sam's house every day. She always had a cheery greeting and a warm smile for Sam. But Sam never managed to get out more than a short "Morning, Miss Richards," or "Evening, Miss Richards."

About 8:30 one summer evening Susan was returning from orchestra practice. She played the violin. As she was passing Sam's house she heard him playing the piano. It wasn't just ordinary playing. It was the work of an artist. Sam was playing snatches from Brahms' great Second Concerto in B flat, a challenge for the very best of musicians. On impulse Susan took her violin out of the case, tuned it softly, and then walked up on the porch and began to play with Sam. Sam was startled, missed a phrase or two, and then moved along. They continued on to a rousing finish.

Did I say finish? That was the beginning, the beginning of a new life for Sam and for Susan. It turned out that Sam was not only a fine musician but an expert linguist as well. I'll never forget the concert Susan and Sam gave in the school auditorium. When the thunderous applause finally died away, Jim Clayton, the chairman of the school board, jumped up on the stage and announced that their search for a man to head the modern language department was over — that is, if Dr. Carter would accept. He did, and his acceptance speech was a masterpiece. Later that evening Susan accepted a proposal from an eloquent musician-linguist. They make a fine couple.

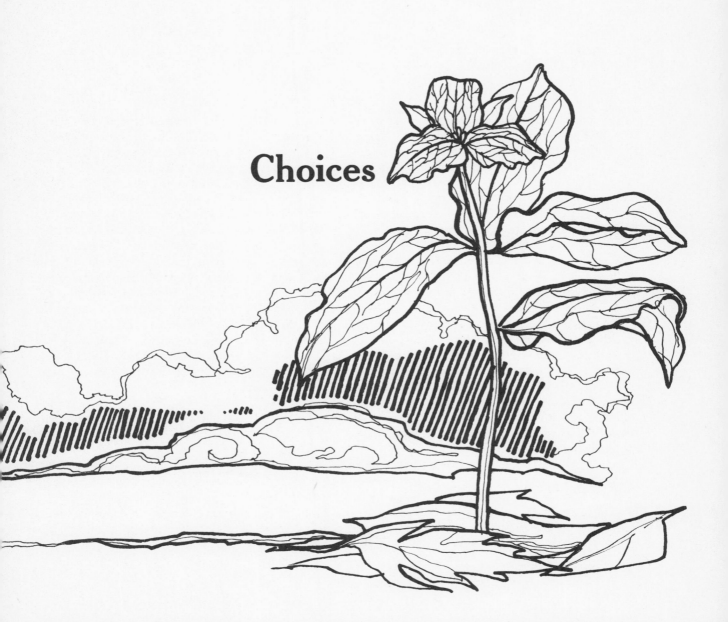

Choices

A Merry Heart

Not many people in our town approved of Jim. You see, Jim never amounted to much, financially that is. Jim never cared about money. And he didn't mind the thinly veiled disapproval of the townspeople. Jim didn't have much money but he had something a great many wealthy people never seem to find. He was the happiest person I've ever known.

When Jim walked into a room he seemed to bring the sunshine with him. His friendly grin and his soft-spoken pleasantries never failed to give a lift to those who were blue.

I remember the last time I talked to Jim. It was Christmas time and I had come home to be with my parents. As I left the station I saw Jim's familiar figure moving along in front of me. His peculiar shuffle made him easily recognizable. I called out to him. He turned and looked my way, his eyes squinting against the falling snow. His half-smile widened as he recognized me.

Jim asked about my new job in the big city, recounted a funny story or two, told me how well I looked and how glad he was to see me. In fact, he steered the conversation toward me and my family in such a way as to make me forget to ask how he was doing. That was the last time I saw him alive. And now, as I recall, he looked terribly thin. Everything about him seemed to have shrunk, except his smile.

Everybody in town attended Jim's funeral. The two banks closed. Only the hospital and power station stayed open — with skeleton staffs. The church couldn't hold the people so the service was moved to the high school auditorium. A stranger might have thought the preacher's text rather odd. I suppose it was. But those who knew Jim knew it was the right one. It was from the seventeenth chapter of Proverbs: "A merry heart is a good medicine . . ." Jim had been dispensing good medicine for years to everybody in town. And all who attended the funeral felt grateful, including those who had not fully approved of him while he was alive.

There are all too many chronic complainers in the world. They are the clouds that obscure the sunshine. Jim was the sunshine that drives away the clouds.

The preacher made a fine talk. However, he could have added one passage of Scripture to make it perfect. It's found in Paul's first letter to Timothy and offers a flawless description of Jim: "Godliness with contentment is great gain."

Brinkmanship

The late John Foster Dulles coined the word *brinkmanship* to describe those periods in a nation's life when it must tread a perilous path on the very brink of war. As we are all well-aware, brinkmanship in our time has become a way of life. This unenviable situation is worldwide and constantly before us. Most of us are vaguely hopeful the ogre will go away, provided we close our eyes and ears to facts. It won't.

However, there is another kind of brinkmanship. Preacher Jones was talking to Del Denning the other day. Del is one of those in-again, out-again, gone-again Christians who try to walk as near to the world as possible and still keep one foot in the church. Usually those who try this delicate balancing act have just enough Christianity to make them miserable. Del was no exception.

The preacher noticed Del had been drinking. He had also heard that Del was having some financial difficulties because of his penchant for playing the horses. And then there were rumors about Del and one of the waitresses in the hotel coffee shop.

As they were talking, Tom Channing, a mutual acquaintance came by, talked for a few moments, and limped on. He had lost a heel and several toes in Vietnam.

Preacher Jones decided to get tough with Del and he began by asking, "Del, are you aware that your limp is even more pronounced than Tom's?"

Del was plainly puzzled. He asked, "What are you talking about, Preacher, I don't limp!"

"But you do, Del," the preacher insisted, "and you're the only one who can't see it." Del asked for an explanation. Preacher Jones whipped out his New Testament, turned to the First Epistle of John and read, "Love not the world, neither the things that are in the world. If any man love the world, the love of the Father is not in him."

"But what's that got to do with me?" Del asked.

"Del, do you think drinking, gambling, and running around are anything other than worldly? And don't you know you're taking a fearful chance? You're on the edge of a deep chasm, limping and staggering. One of these days you're going to fall off and when you do it isn't likely that you'll ever be able to climb back."

Del's face hardened but Preacher Jones looked him right in the eye. In a moment Del softened. "Yeah, you're right," he said, "you're so right. I know I've got to quit acting like this. Believe me, Preacher, I do want to walk straight." And that's just what Del is doing. It's hard for him but not as hard as it was when he was walking so close to the edge.

Elijah's powerful exhortation has special significance for those who dabble in brinkmanship: "How long go ye limping between the two sides? if Jehovah be God, follow him; but if Baal, then follow him."

Advice

Advice is a surplus commodity these days. That isn't anything new; it's always been this way. The reason, I suppose, is that it is so much easier to give advice than to take it.

Nearly three thousand years ago the young son of a great and powerful king was named to the throne of his departed father. The young man called in two sets of advisors. First he talked to the conservatives who counseled, "Your father's rule was heavy. Lighten the heavy rule and the crushing service he imposed upon us and the people will serve you."

Then the king called in the liberals and they advised him to say to the people, "If my father's rule pressed hard on you, I will press harder still; my father lashed you with scourges, but I will lash you with scorpions." You'll find this account in the Book of First Kings.

The advice of the liberals appealed to the young king. When he addressed the people, he really poured it on. He told them that they hadn't seen anything yet; he was really going to make things tough for them. And that was all they needed — to start a revolution.

The young king's name was Rehoboam and he was the son of Solomon. Soon after Rehoboam's speech, the kingdom was divided. The wicked Jeroboam took over the ten tribes of Israel and Rehoboam was left with the tribe of Judah and the tiny tribe of Benjamin.

The power and glory of the united kingdom departed, never to return.

Good advice can be helpful. Bad advice can be harmful and sometimes disastrous. That's why it pays to consider carefully all the issues involved. For example, if Solomon had followed the advice of his father David there would have been a greater heritage for all Israel.

These are the wise words that David directed to his son: "I go the way of all the earth: be thou strong therefore, and shew thyself a man; and keep the charge of the Lord thy God, to walk in his ways, to keep his statutes, and his commandments, and his judgments, and his testimonies, as it is written in the law of Moses, that thou mayest prosper in all that thou doest, and whithersoever thou turnest thyself: That the Lord may continue his word which he spake concerning me, saying, If thy children take heed to their way, to walk before me in truth with all their heart and with all their soul, there shall not fail thee . . . a man on the throne of Israel" (I Kings 2:2-4, *KJV*).

David was a man after God's heart. But it was one greater than David, our Lord and Master, who advised, "Seek ye *first* the kingdom of God, and his righteousness; and all these [material] things shall be added unto you" (Matt. 6:33).

A Humble Christian

"An empty truck makes more noise than a full one."
"An empty head can shatter a tranquil heart." I was reminded
of these old sayings when Rex Redman turned down, with
a great show of piety, an invitation to become an elder
in the church.

I related a story to Rex: A certain man would not consent
to have his name placed before the congregation to serve as
elder. He said, "I drink quite a bit and love to dance.
I am also inclined to gamble and my attendance is not what
it should be. My Bible teaches me that elders should not
do these things. So I would rather be just a faithful,
humble, consecrated member of the church — and let someone
else serve as a elder."

Ah, yes, a faithful, humble, consecrated member of the
church! It wouldn't take very many humble Christians
like that to destroy the church completely.

As the story began to unfold, Redman became, literally,
a red man. But he had the grace to grin and say he deserved
the blow. And I'm glad to say that isn't the end of the
story. Rex turned over not only a new leaf; he turned over
an entire book. He's living for the Lord now, not for himself.
I happen to know his name is coming up again. This time
he's going to answer with a great big affirmative.

The words of John ring with appropriateness today:
"Love not the world, neither the things that are in the world.
If any man love the world, the love of the Father is not
in him" (I John 2:15).

Pull Up, Pull Down

A lovely young girl became infatuated with a fellow who was many spiritual miles removed from her. It was no secret that he drank, he gambled, and, when aroused, which was often because of his low-boiling point, his language was strictly from the gutter.

But the girl was sure she loved him and she was equally sure she could bring about a great reformation in his life and character—which is what she told her preacher. Well, the preacher smiled ruefully as he said, "Sally there's an adage, proved many times over, which young people still refuse to believe."

Naturally, Sally asked what it was.

The preacher replied, "The altar doesn't alter people."

It took a moment to sink in, and then Sally said, "Oh, but this case is different; I'm positive Steve will feel differently about things when we're married."

The preacher shook his head sadly. Then he said, "Sally, hop up on this box." Sally was obviously puzzled but she stepped up on the box. Then the preacher said, "Now, pull me up where you are." Sally tugged but it was impossible for her to pull him up. Then he gave her a slight pull and down she came. The preacher said quietly, "You see, Sally, it's an easy matter for a man to pull a girl down to his level; it's awfully hard for a girl to pull a man up to her level — especially when he isn't interested in attaining her level."

The apostle Paul put the matter clearly and concisely when he said, "Be not unequally yoked with unbelievers: for what fellowship have righteousness and iniquity? or what communion, hath light with darkness . . . or what portion hath a believer with an unbeliever?" (II Cor. 6:14, 15). It was also the apostle Paul who said, "Be not deceived: Evil companionships corrupt good morals" (I Cor. 15:33).

Moral Courage

The other evening I overheard a group of high school boys talking under my office window. They were trying to line up a fellow student in their cause.

It didn't take a Sherlock Holmes . . . (that dates me; let me change detectives). It didn't take an Ironside to discover that the boys were trying hard to get the holdout to help them in a shady deal.

As the discussion grew louder, I found my interest mounting. I deduced that Mr. Jensen, the English teacher, after having given fair warning over a period of several days, had popped an exam that left a number of failures in its wake. And now the boys were out for revenge. They were intent on the malicious destruction of Mr. Jensen's property.

All the boys except Fred were in favor of tinkering with my neighbor's car, activities like pouring sugar in the gas tank.

One of the boys asked, "What's the matter, Fred, are you chicken?"

"No, I'm not chicken," Fred replied, "but if you guys think I'm going to tear up old Jennie's car because I didn't have sense enough to study, you'd better think some more."

Just as Fred was telling off his schoolmates, my neighbor came running down the driveway. He looked nearsightedly at the boys and started talking excitedly. He had broken his glasses and without them he could not see to drive. What's more, he had to get his wife to the hospital — fast.

Fred volunteered to drive. Jensen tossed the keys to him and ran back to the house. Fred could have rubbed it in. He could have said, "D'you guys still want to mess up Jennie's car?" But he didn't say a word. And the silence was pretty heavy. You could almost hear the wheels click as the boys thought of what they had planned to do.

When the teacher came out, half carrying his wife, the ringleader walked up and said, "Mr. Jensen, if there's anything we can do be sure to let us know."

Solomon made a list of the seven things that God hates. Included in the list is "a heart that deviseth wicked purposes" and "feet that are swift in running to mischief."

By the way, Mrs. Jensen is getting along nicely. She enjoyed the flowers sent by Fred and the other boys.

Contentment

"I Don't Got Some"

I remember when Danny was just learning to talk. In spite of the fact that his mother taught English and his father was a writer, one of Danny's oft-heard utterances was, "I don't got some."

Danny's grammatical construction reflected well his attitude. If a playmate suggested a ride on their tricycles, Danny, who did not have one, would respond cheerfully, "I don't got some." And then, quite happily, he would resume playing with some homemade toy.

Danny is a grown man now with children of his own. He doesn't say "I don't got some" these days because, following in his mother's footsteps, he teaches English in the local high school. But there is one thing about Danny that remains unchanged. On those occasions when it becomes necessary for him to admit, to himself or to others, that he doesn't have some of the things that others have, a new car, boat, cottage on the lake, or whatever, he makes the admission as cheerfully as he did about lesser things when he was a boy.

I overheard him talking to his young son the other day. The little fellow was asking for an expensive toy. Danny had to tell him he could not have it. Well, the little fellow burst into tears. At that point Danny preached a fine sermon to his son. It went something like this: "A long time ago in a faraway land there lived a king. The king had everything his heart could desire. Then, one day, he heard about a garden nearby that belonged to a poor man. The king wanted that garden. He wanted very much to have it. But the poor man did not want to sell; it was all he had. Well, the king took the land by force. And the land brought misery and death to the king. The poor man's name was Naboth and the rich king's name was Ahab. Sometimes," Danny concluded, "the things people want most are the very things they should not have."

It was the apostle Paul who said, "I have learned, in whatsoever state I am, therein to be content" (Phil. 4:11).

Self-Sufficiency

John Johnson was probably the strongest man in our town. He wasn't a bad fellow but he had one record, a long-playing one that everybody was sick and tired of hearing. John played it over and over. You see, he was hipped on the subject of his own self-sufficiency.

"Nobody's going to do anything for John Johnson," he was fond of saying. "Old John can take care of himself. He don't ask favors of nobody."

There was more than a grammatical lapse in John's statement. He was dead wrong in thinking he could be completely independent of his fellowmen. It wasn't that John's acquaintances were in sympathy with loafers who made a career of free-loading on others. They just wanted John to stop crowing. Besides, there comes a time in the life of every man when he can't make it alone.

That time came for John much sooner than anyone had anticipated. He awoke one morning feeling as if he had been run over by a truck. He started to get up but couldn't. His legs were paralyzed. "Nonsense," he thought, "I will get up." But he didn't. It took some doing to reach the phone but finally, after a tremendous effort, he made it. Later in the day Doc Brown had to tell John it was polio.

John went all to pieces. He raved and ranted and insisted he was going to get up. He did — and fell flat on his face. It took Doc and three other men to get all two hundred and ninety-five pounds of him back on the bed.

I'm sure John would have starved to death if the neighbors hadn't brought in food after he was discharged from the hospital. Even so, he must have lost fifty pounds. And he kept going down. Then Jim Rankin, the preacher, brought John some food that changed things. John didn't take it willingly, but he took it.

The preacher came in one morning and said, "John, I have something here I want you to swallow."

"Don't want it," John said.

"Want it or not, I've brought it to you and you're going to take it." Then he opened his Bible and began to read. I don't know how many passages he read, but I do know he ended the reading with two short statements from Jeremiah and the Psalms. The one in Jeremiah says, "O Lord, I know that the way of man is not in himself: it is not in man that walketh to direct his steps." The verse in Psalms is, "Cast thy burden upon the Lord, and he shall sustain thee: he shall never suffer the righteous to be moved."

That was the turning point. John is making it under his own power these days. Physically he isn't so much but mentally and spiritually — well, all I can say is, John Johnson is quite a man.

The Failure

Bill Clay runs a little farm. He also fills in at the local high school when the teaching situation gets desperate, which is fairly often. Bill even preaches occasionally when the parson is sick or out of town.

Bill can do just about anything, anything that is, as Jim Newton the town banker was saying the other day, except make money. Jim warmed to his subject with righteous indignation: "Talk about a failure — Bill Clay could be in a class with the wealthiest men this town has ever produced if he were to put his mind to it. He ought to be in Nashville, or New York, or Chicago. But what does he do? I'll tell you what he does. He stays in a one-horse town on a one-horse farm and makes just about enough to feed one horse — only he doesn't have a horse; he's got a little beat-up tractor." Jim then went on to name several who started out about the time Bill did — fellows who since then had made it big.

Doc Sudberry was listening to the banker's tirade. When Jim paused to take a breath, old Doc said, "I've been keeping up with the big wheels you've been talking about. I talked to Roger's psychiatrist last week; he says it will probably take a year or so for Roger to get back on his feet — if he's lucky. And by the way, Jim, did you know John is nursing a duo-denal ulcer? And did you hear the news about Tom, the wheeler-dealer everybody's talking about? His wife is divorcing him — says she thought she was marrying a man but he turned out to be a robot. According to her story, they've had one meal together in the past six weeks. This fellow Bill Clay that you've been giving such a hard time, have you heard the latest on him?"

"No," Jim said, "can't say that I have."

"Well, I'll tell you about that poor old failure: He has an enormous appetite and a huge freezer that's chock full of vegetables and meat that he has raised himself. Nancy, his pretty wife, worships the ground he walks on. Bill has plenty of time to take his kids fishin' and huntin'. He sleeps like a baby, doesn't have a worry in the world, and I've never seen him when he wasn't in a happy frame of mind. Yeah, Bill Clay is a terrible failure."

A long time ago the wise man Solomon prayed, "Feed me with the food that is needful for me: Lest I be full, and deny thee, and say, Who is Jehovah? Or lest I be poor, and steal, And use profanely the name of my God." It was this same wise man who observed, "Better it is to be of a lowly spirit with the poor, than to divide the spoil with the proud . . . whoso trusteth in Jehovah, happy is he."

Old Million

Have you read the Book of Ecclesiastes lately? I was reading it last night. Now there is a book for the jet age!

We like to think that nothing escapes the minute probing of modern research. Whether it be the other side of the moon or the inside of a man's brain, the searching goes on. And with regard to human conduct it seems, of late, that no question is too personal.

All of this makes Solomon a pretty modern fellow, even though he lived nearly three thousand years ago. His words are a combination of bright inspiration tinged with bitter experience. He clearly and pointedly details the vanity of world-centered aspirations. And his message sums up the hard fact that material achievement, apart from moral integrity, is utterly futile.

Let me tell you about Merrit Milden. He doesn't know it but his nickname is "Million." Old Million has a beautiful mansion and an exquisite garden (that requires a full-time gardener), a house in Florida, and a cabin in Maine. He probably has more money than he could conveniently count, even with the help of his staff — a rather large staff for a man who says he has retired.

Million is a bitter and lonely man. He's a bachelor. He always said he was afraid women were after his money. Maybe they were. There isn't much to be said in favor of a man who doesn't trust anybody.

Solomon said, ". . . I gathered me . . . silver and gold, and the treasure of kings and of the provinces . . . so I was great, and increased more than all that were before me . . ." (Eccles. 2:8, 9). And his conclusion? "All was vanity and a striving after wind, and there was no profit under the sun" (Eccles. 2:11).

It would be well, after reading Solomon's morose statement, to consider these words from Paul: "Godliness with contentment is great gain: for we brought nothing into the world, for neither can we carry anything out; but having food and covering we shall be therewith content" (I Tim. 6: 6, 7).

Family

Opposite

Clayton Carleton was a big, self-assured man. People said of him that he knew his way around and that nothing and nobody could stand in the way of his success. He had all the things he had longed for in his youth, and more. Money? He had plenty. A beautiful home? Yes. Powerful automobiles? A cabin in the mountains? A cottage by the seashore? He had all of these and he also had a beautiful wife and two fine little boys.

One night after dinner he overheard the boys playing a game they called "Opposite." If one wanted a knife, he asked for a fork. If one said "smile," the other was supposed to scowl.

The game set Carleton to thinking about his own life. Several times he had been guilty of subterfuge and misrepresentation when the success of a big deal was at stake. On those occasions he had prided himself on his ability to maintain a poker face. Later, the face of a confused competitor or perhaps someone in his own organization returned to

haunt him. There was Jones, for example. Jones had trusted him implicitly, but he had let Jones down. He told himself it was for the good of the company. Jones had a complete breakdown when he lost his job and his son had to quit college. Carleton's partner had shrugged off the incident. "Stop worrying," he said, "Jones was just a weak sister."

After the boys had gone upstairs to bed, Carleton picked up the Bible. He turned to the fifth chapter of Isaiah. "Woe unto them that call evil good, and good evil;" he read, "that put darkness for light, and light for darkness; that put bitter for sweet, and sweet for bitter. Woe unto them that are wise in their own eyes, and prudent in their own sight" (Isa. 5:20, 21, *KJV*).

It was a chastened father who said gently to his children the next morning at breakfast, "Boys, I would rather you didn't play 'Opposite.' It makes me think of a game that I've been playing, a game I do not intend to play again — ever!"

In Loving Memory

In the Grayson family plot there is an old-fashioned inscription: "In loving memory of our dear father." And then in bold letters is the name "Randolph Grayson, 1893-1973."

Randy Grayson was buried last year at the age of eighty. But he died twenty-five years ago. Not actually, of course, but it has been twenty-five years since he was committed to the State Hospital. He was fifty-five then and he had been working almost day and night for years, trying to provide for his demanding, unthoughtful, avaricious family. When Randy escaped into that dim world called insanity, he was carted off to the asylum with little ceremony and with even less feeling.

Through the years his two sons and three daughters just couldn't find time to visit their father. But last week they all showed up at the funeral. You've never seen such mourn-ing. A quartet sang "Beautiful Isle of Somewhere." The eulogies were heartwarming and the flowers were gorgeous. It was all very beautiful — and sad and hypocritical. Too bad some of those lovely tributes were not given before Randy's heart and spirit were broken a little over twenty-five years ago.

There are a great many Randy Graysons in this old world; they are in desperate need of pleasant words and friends who take the time to show they care.

Solomon was speaking from experience as well as inspiration when he said, "By sorrow of heart the spirit is broken." He knew about certain restorative and healing powers, long before the discovery of wonder drugs. "Pleasant words," said this ancient wise man, "are as a honeycomb, sweet to the soul, and health to the bones" (Prov. 16:24).

Honor Thy Father and Thy Mother

"What do we live for, if not to make life happier and less difficult for each other?" That question was asked a long time ago by George Eliot. And Hugh Parrish, known locally as Bully, had the answer. Bully lived for himself. Moreover, he didn't make any bones about it. "Sure I put myself first," he was fond of saying, "if ya don't look out for number-one, nobody else will."

Bully was nearing fifty years of age when he decided to place his parents in a rest home in town. There was nothing especially wrong with the home; it was just the matter of how Bully's parents felt about leaving the farm.

Bully didn't even bother to drive the old folks to town. As he bundled his crippled father and his ailing mother into the station wagon the driver, Jim Tully, heard Mrs. Parrish say, "But, Hugh, please, we don't want to leave the farm." Jim said it made him sick at the stomach.

"I know, Mom," Bully said hurriedly, "but I've got a million things to do here at the farm and besides, you'll be much more comfortable at Sunnydale." His dad didn't say a word. He just held his head up proudly. As the station wagon pulled off the old man gave Bully a long look. There was no hatred in his eyes — just pity.

I guess the worst part of the whole affair was the fact that Bully could have provided round-the-clock nursing care, had it been necessary, and never missed the extra expense. Oh, how much his parents wanted to spend their last days on their beloved farm!

About three weeks later Bully's oldest boy, who was home from college for spring vacation, tossed a cigarette aside while he was working in the new barn. The fire must have smoldered a long time. About midnight a blaze sprang up. A high wind did the rest. By the time the volunteer fire department arrived, the barn was a total loss, and the owner of the barn was in critical condition.

When Bully awakened and saw the barn enveloped in flames, he thought of his registered cattle, his new tractor, his combine. He frantically dashed out of the house on a dead run toward the barn. But he never made it. I believe the doctor called it a massive coronary occlusion. He was dead on arrival at the hospital.

At the funeral it was hard to concentrate on the service. I kept thinking of the words of George Eliot, and the Scriptural commandment: "Honor thy father and thy mother that thy days may be long upon the land which the Lord thy God giveth thee."

Little Girl Lost

Linda and her mother were walking down busy Woodward Avenue. It was a lovely day, unseasonably warm for late fall. Linda was five years old and thrilled over the prospect of a day of shopping with her mother, lunch at a big department store, and a Walt Disney movie in the afternoon.

Linda's mother was happy too. Her husband's new job was shaping up well. The big city was fascinating. And Linda was such a joy. "Hurry, Linda," she called, "I don't want to lose you."

Linda didn't answer and her mother turned around. The little girl was nowhere in sight. Hundreds, no thousands, of people were rushing, pushing, hurrying, but no Linda.

A wave of fear swept over the young mother. "She was here a few seconds ago," she told herself, "I must not panic." But she did. She suffered agonies as the minutes ticked by. She ran frantically back down the street, calling her daughter's name, heedless of the cold stares of the people who brushed against her.

What should she do? Where should she go? Where could her child be? How terribly frightened she was — and, she thought, how frightened her little girl must be.

Just then a police prowl car came slowly by. A little girl was sitting on the lap of a policeman. She was eating an ice cream cone and looking out the window. "Hello, Mama," she called blithely, "I'm riding wif a ossifer."

The mother hugged her daughter close. Tears streamed down her cheeks as she thanked the policemen. One of them grinned and said, "It happens all the time, lady."

"It happens all the time." But what of the lost who are never found? This is all too true in the realm of the spirit. In Jesus' story of the prodigal the father said gratefully, "This thy brother was . . . lost, and is found!"

How frightening to be lost. How tragic to be lost forever.

Apathy

Tom Smith came slowly out of the fog as the insistent buzzing of his alarm clock shattered a beautiful dream in which he was basking on a warm, sunny beach. With a groan he turned off the alarm and slid one foot out of the covers to the floor. Tom's other foot almost hit the floor, but not quite. Said Tom to Tom, "This is Sunday, you nut, you don't have to get up!"

The pedal extremities quickly returned to the warm spot under the covers. Tom stretched long and luxuriously and gratefully. Then he heard the blip-blip of the percolator and almost immediately he sniffed the delicious aroma of coffee. Tom was sure his Nancy could make better coffee than television's Mrs. Olson.

Nancy came in, set a cup of steaming coffee on the night table, opened the morning paper and made a mock curtsey. "Now," she said, her adorable dimple deepening as she grinned, "does my master require anything more?"

"I'll try to think of something," Tom said as he sat up and bunched a pillow behind his back. As Nancy disappeared through the bedroom door Tom mused, "Boy, I've really got it made." "It" included, in addition to his lovely wife, two good-looking, intelligent boys, aged six and eight, a ranch style house on a five-acre plot, a job to his liking, and a dream office downtown.

Best of all, Tom had plenty of time to indulge his hobbies — fishing and boating in summer, woodworking in winter. And on this wintry morning Tom began to think of that marvelous supply of mahogany he had picked up the week before during a trip upstate. He grinned appreciatively as he sipped his coffee. The old farmer had insisted that he take it and was equally insistent about not taking any pay for it.

Tom turned to the feature section. There was a picture of several noted churchmen. Tom's roving eye remained on the tableau just long enough to read the caption, "Religious Leaders Label Apathy Church's Greatest Foe." Tom thumbed some more. He read the sports pages thoroughly before tossing the paper aside.

The telephone rang. Tom could hear Nancy's "hello" in the kitchen. His buzzer sounded. Who could be calling at this hour on Sunday? "Hello," he growled.

"Hi, Tom, this is Andy Jones. Say, I'm on the church attendance committee. Where have you been hiding? Anything wrong?"

"No, nothing's wrong." There was an awkward pause and Tom found it necessary to add, "Been pretty busy lately . . . we'll make it sometime soon."

"Today?"

"No, not today, but one of these times soon."

"OK, Tom, just checking."

Tom hung up just as Nancy walked in. "What was that all about?" she asked.

"Andy Jones is after me about not going to church."

"Oh? And why don't we go to church? We used to — all the time."

"Yeah, but that was before we . . ." Tom's voice trailed off.

"Before we struck it rich?"

"What are you doing, Nan, preaching to me?"

"Yes, I think so." A frown replaced Nancy's smile. "Last night I was reading the Bible to the children for the first time in ages and one of the passages I read disturbs me."

"What was that?"

"It was in Proverbs, something about 'He that trusteth in riches shall fall; but the righteous shall flourish.' "

"So?"

"So what do you suppose Jimmy asked?"

"What?"

"He asked, 'Mama, does that mean we can't get everything we want with money?' " Nancy looked searchingly at her husband. "That's a pretty big question Tom. Think about it."

As Nancy walked away Tom felt vaguely disturbed. Thoughts of other years, the struggling years, danced through his mind — Sunday worship, mid-week meetings, times when he had spoken in the preacher's absence, friends who used to drop in after church. What was it the religious leaders had said? He fumbled through the newspaper, found the page, and began reading under the caption, "Religious Leaders Label Apathy Church's Greatest Foe."

Goin' Home

Cindy made a decision to go home and that decision almost broke up the show in which she was appearing. It was opening night and when her cue came she just stood there smiling sadly, tears glistening in her eyes. The emcee covered up for her with an outlandish story. The waves of laughter rocked Cindy back to the business at hand. She took her cue and sang beautifully.

Cynthia Beauregard came to New York from a little town in South Carolina. When she left a very musical home, she said some ugly things to her mother and dad. That was years ago, long before she came to be recognized as a remarkable singer.

Through the years Cindy achieved just about everything she had set out to do. But more and more she was gripped by a feeling of emptiness. The harder she drove herself, the worse the feeling became. Then it happened! The night the musical opened a short bit was added as an introduction to Cindy's song. It was only a few bars from the largo of Dvorak's New World Symphony: "Goin' home . . . I'm just goin' home."

Cindy was lost for a moment. She had been thinking all day of how much she wanted to see her mother and father. And right there on the stage, before a crowded house, tears came to her eyes and she missed her cue. When she did sing, though, she brought down the house. It was beautiful. And that was her last appearance for two weeks. She went home — that night. Her understudy had to take over. And when Cindy returned she was better than ever.

Later a critic asked Cindy what she was thinking during those long moments while the orchestra leader and everybody else in the house looked at her in amazement. Cindy said simply, "I was thinking of when I was a little girl and how my mother played the piano. While I struggled with the cello, Dad played the violin. I was also thinking of how we used to play 'Goin' home.' I decided right then and there that if they would have me I was going home and beg them to forgive me for the way I had treated them."

"Did they?" the critic asked.

Cindy smiled and handed him a small New Testament. "The answer to your question is found in the fifteenth chapter of Luke."

"The fifteenth chapter of Luke . . . what are you talking about?" the critic sputtered.

"Just turn and read the part I have marked."

He did, and he understood; it was the story of the prodigal. Jesus' parable tells of the prodigal's return and of the father who was moved with compassion, joyfully welcoming him home.

The Time Is Now

John Davidson is a real estate broker. He is also, as of last week, a cattleman.

When John's dad heard about his son's new venture in livestock he took the young man to task. "John," he said, reprovingly, "you're stretching it too thin. You ought to wait until things are more settled before you make such moves. There's too much danger now. Besides, you'll be in better shape to take on extra activities when you get your business well-oiled and running smoothly. There's plenty of time," he added, "without jumping into something about which you know so little right now."

"Dad," John asked, "haven't you told me time and again that you always wanted to find a little place and raise chickens?"

"Well, yes, but what's that got to do. . . ."

"Dad," John persisted, "do you realize you've been talking about it for twenty years?"

"That's true, son, but . . ."

"But the truth of the matter, Dad, is that you're no nearer to it now than you were twenty years ago. Right?"

It was apparent that John's dad was forming a sharp retort. But instead he grinned sheepishly and said, "John, you go right ahead with your livestock. And, John, do you have a listing down at the office of a few acres that I could turn into a chicken farm?"

Procrastination is a wily thief of that precious commodity called time. And time is of utmost importance in the spiritual realm. Remember Felix who was frightened by the preaching of Paul. The apostle's theme was righteousness, self-control, and the judgment to come. So Felix was terrified and he said to Paul, "Go thy way for this time; and when I have a convenient season, I will call thee unto me" (Acts 24:25). There is no record that Felix ever found a convenient season.

". . . Now is the acceptable time; behold, now is the day of salvation" (II Cor. 6:2).

"I Want a Conscience"

A mother and her three-year-old daughter were watching a television program on which the word *conscience* was used. The little girl repeated the word and then, in the manner of little girls, she repeated it a great many times.

Later, long after the television had been turned off, the mother was startled to hear her little one pronounce the word again. She was just a little chagrined to hear the child say, "Me want a conscience."

The mother confided, "My little Gwen asked for something I can't give her, but perhaps I can be helpful in educating the conscience the Lord gave her."

Conscience is not infallible. The apostle Paul admitted that his conscience was clear, even when he was guilty of opposing the Mas-ter (Acts 23:1). Recently I heard about the Italian bandit whose conscience was clear because he had never murdered anybody on Sunday!

Conscience, in order to be effective must be nurtured by the Word of God. Anything short of divine guidance can render one's conscience completely worthless.

The apostle Paul tells of a time that will produce sinful, hypocritical men "that speak lies, branded in their own conscience as with a hot iron" (I Tim. 4:2). In another place he speaks of those "who being past feeling gave themselves up to lasciviousness, to work all uncleanness with greediness" (Eph. 4:19). On the other hand, this same apostle extols the virtue of "a good conscience and faith unfeigned" (I Tim. 1:5).

Crazy Bill

They called him Crazy Bill. An injury received in childhood gave his mouth a wicked looking grimace that was enough to scare anyone who didn't know him. And then there was the way he walked; he loped along with a peculiar shuffling gait that children loved to mimic.

Bill was probably as well read as anybody in town but he didn't have much to say — except to Ginny Brown. Five-year-old Ginny insisted that Bill was her very best friend.

The little house where Bill lived bordered on the Allison Brown property. Allison was president of the First City Bank. He had to drive past Bill's place every day, going to and from his palatial house on the hill. Allison had tried everything short of a shotgun to get Bill to sell out but Bill steadfastly refused. He said the house had been in his family for generations and, since he was the last of the line, he just couldn't sell. But Allison never quit trying. He said and did all sorts of mean things that made life miserable for Crazy Bill. But Ginny, Allison's little girl, liked Bill from the very first time she saw him.

One day Ginny was playing at the edge of the Brown's swimming pool. Just as she gave a friendly wave to Bill, who was shuffling by, her foot slipped and in she went.

Allison drove up just in time to see Crazy Bill dive awkwardly into the water. By the time he got out of the car and raced over to the pool Bill was depositing Ginny on the edge of the pool, coughing and scared, but none the worse for her experience.

Allison didn't even look at Bill as he held Ginny tight and kissed her. But Ginny pulled away and called to Bill who was moving away. "Thank you, Mr. Bill," she said. Bill turned, grinned crookedly, and began to shuffle off. Instead he sank to the ground. He was dead when Dr. Ramsey arrived. Doc said it was a heart attack.

That was when Allison Brown, who prided himself on being tough, found out he wasn't so tough. On the day of the funeral he asked if he might read a passage of Scripture. His voice shook as he read the familiar lines, "Greater love hath no man than this, that a man lay down his life for his friend." "Ginny was Bill's friend," he said brokenly, "I regret that I was not."

It was the apostle Paul who said, "Be not overcome of evil, but overcome evil with good."